TRUSTS OF LAND –
THE NEW LAW

TRUSTS OF LAND AND APPOINTMENT
OF TRUSTEES ACT 1996

TRUSTS OF LAND –
THE NEW LAW
TRUSTS OF LAND AND APPOINTMENT
OF TRUSTEES ACT 1996

Angela Sydenham MA, LLB
Solicitor with Birketts, Ipswich

with precedents prepared by
Colin Sydenham MA
Barrister

JORDANS

1996

Published by
Jordan Publishing Limited
21 St Thomas Street
Bristol BS1 6JS

British Library Cataloguing-in-Publication Data
A catalogue record for this book is available from the British Library.

ISBN 0 85308 395 9

Typeset by Mendip Communications Ltd, Frome, Somerset
Printed in Great Britain by Biddles Ltd, Guildford and King's Lynn

DEDICATION

To my beneficiaries

Colin, Simon, Rupert
and Katy

PREFACE

The office of *Cestui que Trust*
Is reserved for the learned and just
Any villain you choose
May be *Cestui que Use*
But a lawyer for Cestui que Trust

Cautionary Tales – H Belloc
Obiter Dicta

So wrote Belloc. Of course *cestui que trust* and *cestui que use* both mean beneficiary. The reference in the first line to *cestui que trust* should be to *feoffee que trust*.

There is no doubt that the Trusts of Land and Appointment of Trustees Act 1996 is lawyer's law. Although there are changes in terminology, its application is not likely to be startling. Most of the provisions merely record what happens in practice. Very few people today deliberately create strict settlements. Most properly drawn trust documents give the trustees the powers of an absolute owner. Even the provisions for the beneficiaries to be able to give directions for the appointment and retirement of trustees apply only where the beneficiaries are unanimous and are in a position to terminate the trust.

There will be many who will see the legislation as unnecessary and meddlesome. On the whole, practitioners have coped with the dual system of a strict settlement and trust for sale. They have not seemed unduly troubled by the imposition of a statutory trust for sale where there is co-ownership. The problems may have been more apparent to academics and those in the business of law reform.

Nevertheless, the Act makes trusts of land more logical. In giving greater flexibility to trustees, more rights to beneficiaries and clearer powers to the court, the Act should benefit all interested parties and their advisers.

This book looks at the Act from the position of the trustees, the beneficiaries, the purchaser and the court. This inevitably means that there is some repetition in the text. It is not expected, however, that there will be many readers who will want to read the book straight through. For those who distrust other people's interpretation of legislation, the Trusts of Land and Appointment of Trustees Act 1996 is set out fully in Appendix I. The annotations are intended to be helpful, but can be disregarded.

My husband has provided the precedents, for which I am truly thankful. He cannot, however, be held responsible for any inaccuracies in the text which he has not seen. It is hoped that by having precedents, this publication will prove to be a really useful book for practitioners.

Special thanks are due to Peggy Alexander, my secretary. She has dealt with the many amendments and rewrites with good humour and efficiency. Also, I am grateful to Martin West of Jordans who suggested I wrote the book in the first place and who from time to time encouraged me with luncheons, and Mollie Dickenson, my helpful editor.

Finally, thank you to Birketts, the Ipswich Solicitors, who employed me late in life and allowed me to scribble in office time.

The law is stated as at 31 August 1996.

ANGELA SYDENHAM
Michaelmas

CONTENTS

Preface   vii
Table of Cases   xiii
Table of Statutes   xv
Table of Statutory Instruments   xix
Glossary   xxi

Chapter 1   THE NEED FOR LEGISLATION   1
             1.1   Introduction   1
             1.2   The Dual System   1
             1.3   Bare Trusts   8
             1.4   Background to the Reform   8

Chapter 2   APPLICATION AND OUTLINE OF THE TRUSTS OF
             LAND AND APPOINTMENT OF TRUSTEES ACT 1996   11
             2.1   Application   11
             2.2   Outline   11

Chapter 3   TRUSTS OF LAND   21
             3.1   Meaning of Trust of Land   21
             3.2   Creation of Trust of Land   21
             3.3   Strict Settlements   22
             3.4   Universities and College Estates Act 1925   26
             3.5   The Chequers and Chevening Estates   26
             3.6   Express Trusts for Sale   27
             3.7   Statutory Trust for Sale   27
             3.8   Points for Practitioners   29

Chapter 4   APPOINTMENT AND RETIREMENT OF TRUSTEES   31
             4.1   Introduction   31
             4.2   Appointment of Initial Trustees   32
             4.3   Appointment of Subsequent Trustees   32
             4.4   Who May Make the Appointment?   34
             4.5   Direction by the Beneficiaries to Appoint
                    Trustees   35
             4.6   Direction for Replacement Trustee   35
             4.7   Direction for the Retirement of a Trustee   35
             4.8   Protection of a Retiring Trustee   36
             4.9   Rules on Directions   37
             4.10   Points for Practitioners   37

Chapter 5   POWERS OF TRUSTEES   39
             5.1   Introduction   39
             5.2   Powers of an Absolute Owner   39
             5.3   Power to Sell or Retain Land   40
             5.4   Power to Convey Land to a Beneficiary   41
             5.5   Power to Purchase Land   42
             5.6   Power to Petition   43
             5.7   Limitations on Powers   44
             5.8   Power to Delegate   48
             5.9   Personal Representatives   53
             5.10   Points for Practitioners   53

Chapter 6   POWERS OF THE COURT   55
             6.1   Limitations of section 30 of the Law of Property
                    Act 1925   55
             6.2   Who May Make an Application   56
             6.3   The Powers   56
             6.4   Appointment or Removal of Trustees   57
             6.5   Determination of Applications   57
             6.6   Insolvency   58

Chapter 7   POSITION OF BENEFICIARIES   61
             7.1   Meaning of Beneficiary   61
             7.2   Previous Law   61
             7.3   Position Strengthened   62
             7.4   Interest in Land Rather Than Proceeds of Sale   62
             7.5   Right of Occupation   63
             7.6   Trustees' Obligations to Beneficiaries   67
             7.7   Directions to Trustees   69
             7.8   Enforced Termination of the Trust   70
             7.9   Power to Apply to the Court   70
             7.10   Points for Practitioners   71

Chapter 8   PROTECTION OF THE PURCHASER   73
             8.1   Introduction   73
             8.2   Overreaching   73
             8.3   Purchasers Not Concerned With All Trustees'
                    Obligations   75
             8.4   Protection Where Trustees' Powers Delegated   77
             8.5   Termination of the Trust   77
             8.6   Charitable, Ecclesiastical and Public Trusts   78
             8.7   Points for Practitioners   79

Appendix I   Trusts of Land and Appointment of Trustees Act
                    1996   81

Appendix II   Parliamentary Stages of the Trustees of Land and
                  Appointment of Trustees Act   131

Appendix III   Checklists and Precedents   133

Index   157

TABLE OF CASES

References are to paragraph numbers except where they are in *italics* which are references to page numbers.

Atkins' Will Trusts, Re [1974] 1 WLR 761, 118 SJ 391, *sub nom* Atkins' Will Trusts,
    Re; National Westminster Bank v Atkins [1974] 2 All ER 1   3.6

Barclay v Barclay [1970] 2 QB 677, [1970] 3 WLR 82, [1970] 2 All ER 676, CA   1.2.5, 7.4,
     7.5.1, *92*
Beaumont Settled Estates, Re [1937] 2 All ER 353   1.2.4
Bedson v Bedson [1965] 2 QB 66, [1965] 3 WLR 891, [1965] 3 All ER 307, CA   5.3
Brockbank, Re, Ward v Bates [1948] Ch 206, [1948] 1 All ER 287, [1948] LJR 952   4.3, *98*
Buchanan-Wollaston's Conveyance, Re; Curtis v Buchanan-Wollaston [1939] Ch
     738, [1939] 2 All ER 302, 108 LJ Ch 281, CA   5.3
Bull v Bull [1955] 1 QB 234, [1955] 2 WLR 78, [1955] 1 All ER 253, CA   1.2.4, 1.2.5, 7.4,
     7.5.1, *92*
Burke v Burke [1974] 1 WLR 1063, [1974] 2 All ER 944, (1973) 118 SJ 98, CA   6.5.1
Buttle v Saunders [1950] 2 All ER 193, [1950] WN 255, 66 TLR (Pt 1) 1026   5.7.2

Cedar Holdings Ltd v Green and Another [1981] Ch 129, [1979] 3 WLR 31, [1979] 3
     All ER 117, CA   1.2.5, 7.4
Cooper v Critchley [1955] Ch 431, [1955] 2 WLR 510, [1955] 1 All ER 520, CA   1.2.5, 7.4

Dennis v McDonald [1982] Fam 63, [1982] 2 WLR 275, [1982] 1 All ER 590, CA   7.5.1
Duce and Boots Cash Chemists (Southern) Ltd's Contract, Re [1937] Ch 642,
     [1937] 3 All ER 788, 106 LJ Ch 387   1.2.6

Elias v Mitchell [1972] Ch 652, [1972] 2 WLR 740, [1972] 2 All ER 153   1.2.5, 7.4
England v Public Trustee (1968) 112 SJ 70, 117 New LJ 1321, 205 EG 651, CA   1.2.3, 7.2

Herklot's Wills Trust, Re, Temple v Scorer [1964] 1 WLR 583, [1964] 2 All ER 66,
     108 SJ 424   1.2.6
Holliday (A Bankrupt), Re; ex parte Trustee of the Bankrupt v The Bankrupt
     [1981] Ch 405, [1981] 2 WLR 996, [1980] 3 All ER 385, CA   5.3

Irani Finance v Singh [1971] Ch 59, [1970] 3 WLR 330, [1970] 3 All ER 199, CA   1.2.5, 7.4

Jones v Challenger [1961] 1 QB 176, [1960] 2 WLR 695, [1960] 1 All ER 785, CA   5.3
Jones (AE) v Jones (FW) [1977] 1 WLR 438, (1976) 33 P & CR 147, (1976) 242 EG
     371, CA   1.2.5, 7.4

Keech v Sandford (1726) Sel Cas t King 61, 2 Wh & Tud LC 693   5.7.2
Kempthorne, Re; Charles v Kempthorne [1930] 1 Ch 268, [1929] All ER Rep 495, 99
  LJ Ch 177, CA   1.2.5, 7.4

Leigh's Settled Estates (No 1) [1926] Ch 852, [1926] All ER Rep 688, 95 LJ Ch 511   1.2.6
Lowrie, Re, ex parte Trustee of the Bankrupt v The Bankrupt [1981] 3 All ER 353, DC   5.3
Luke v South Kensington Hotel Co (1879) 11 Ch D 121, [1874-80] All ER Rep
  1293, 48 LJ Ch 361, CA   5.7.2

Mayo, Re; Mayo v Mayo [1943] Ch 302, [1943] 2 All ER 440, 112 LJ Ch 257   3.8.2, 5.3, *85,*
                                                                                    152

National Westminster Bank v Allen [1971] 2 QB 718, [1971] 3 WLR 495, [1971] 3 All
  ER 201n   1.2.5, 7.4
Norton, Re; Pinney v Beauchamp [1929] 1 Ch 84, [1928] All ER Rep 301, 98 LJ
  Ch 219   1.2.4

Parker's Settled Estates, Re; Parker v Parker [1928] Ch 247, [1927] All ER Rep
  546, 97 LJ Ch 161   1.2.4
Pearson v IRC [1981] AC 753, [1980] 2 WLR 872, [1980] 2 All ER 479, HL   5.8.2
Pennant's Will Trusts, Re; Pennant v Rylands [1970] Ch 75, [1969] 3 WLR 63,
  [1969] 2 All ER 862   1.2.3
Perry v Phoenix Assurance [1988] 1 WLR 940, [1988] 3 All ER 60, (1988) 56 P &
  CR 163   7.4
Power's Will Trusts, Re; Public Trustee v Hastings [1947] Ch 572, [1947] 2 All ER
  282, 91 SJ 409   5.5

Rawlings v Rawlings [1964] P 398, [1964] 3 WLR 294, [1964] 2 All ER 804, CA   6.5.1
Rooke, Re; Rooke v Rooke [1953] Ch 716, [1953] 2 WLR 1176, sub nom Rooke's
  Will Trusts, Re, Taylor v Rooke [1953] 2 All ER 110   3.6
Ryder and Steadman's Contract, Re [1927] 2 Ch 62, [1927] All ER Rep 506, 96 LJ
  Ch 388, CA   1.2.4

Saunders v Vautier (1841) 4 Beav 115, [1835-42] All ER Rep 58, 10 LJ Ch 354   4.3, 7.8, *98,*
                                                                                    107
Sharpe's Deed of Release, Re; Sharpe and Fox v Gullick [1939] Ch 51, [1938] 3
  All ER 449, 54 TLR 1039   1.2.4
Spearman Settled Estates, Re [1906] 2 Ch 502   4.5
Speight v Gaunt (1883) 9 App Cas 1, 53 LJ Ch 419, 50 LT 330, HL   5.7.2

Thornhill's Settlement, Re [1941] Ch 24, [1940] 4 All ER 249, 111 LJ Ch 5, CA   1.2.3

Wakeman, Re; National Provincial Bank v Wakeman [1945] Ch 177, [1945] 1 All
  ER 421, 114 LJ Ch 145   5.5
Wellsted's Will Trusts, Re, Wellsted v Hanson [1949] Ch 296, [1949] 1 All ER 577,
  [1949] LJR 1153, CA   5.5
Williams (JW) v Williams (MA) [1976] Ch 278, [1976] 3 WLR 494, [1977] 1 All
  ER 28, CA   6.5.1
Williams & Glyn's Bank Ltd v Boland [1981] AC 487, [1980] 2 All ER 408   1.2.5, 7.4

TABLE OF STATUTES

References are to paragraph numbers except where they are in *italics* which are references to page numbers.

3 and 4 Anne, c 6 (1704)	*102*
5 Anne, c 3 (1706)	*102*
54 Geo 3, c 161 (1814)	*102*
Administration of Estates Act 1925	
s 22	1.2.3
s 33	3.7.3, *111*
s 51(3)	3.3.5
Agricultural Tenancies Act 1995	
s 33	5.2
Agriculture Act 1970	
s 30(2)	*103*
Charging Orders Act 1979	7.4
Charities Act 1993	3.3.4, 8.6
s 36	3.3.4
(1)	*107*
s 37	3.3.4, *96, 107*
(1),(2)	8.6, *107*
(3)	*107*
s 38	3.3.4
s 39	3.3.4, *96, 107*
(1),(2)	8.6
Children Act 1989	7.6.3, *91*
Coast Protection Act 1949	
s 11(2)	5.2
Domestic Violence and Matrimonial Proceedings Act 1976	7.5.1
Enduring Powers of Attorney Act 1985	2.2.6, 2.2.13, 5.8.2
Family Law Reform Act 1969	
Sch 3 para 6	5.7.5
Family Law Reform Act 1987	*90*
Hill Farming Act 1946	
s 11(2)	5.2

Inheritance Tax Act 1984	
s 237(3)	7.4
Insolvency Act 1986	2.2.10, 6.6, *95*
s 355A	5.3
(2)–(4)	6.6
Land Charges Act 1972	7.4
Land Registration Act 1925	
s 20	8.2.1, 8.5.3
s 70(1)(g)	8.2.1, 8.5.3
s 86	*87*
(2)	8.2.1
Landlord and Tenant Act 1927	
s 13	5.2
Landlord and Tenant Act 1954	
Sch 2 para 6	5.2
Law of Property Act 1925	1.2.4, 1.2.5, 1.2.7, 3.6, *83, 90, 102, 103*
Pt I	8.1
s 1(6)	1.2.1
s 2	8.1, 8.2.1
s 7(1)	3.3.6
s 15	*139*
s 19	3.3.1, *106*
s 20	4.2
s 23	*86*
s 25	3.6, *85*
s 26	*90*
(2)	*90*
(3)	5.7.5, 7.2, 7.6.4, *91*
s 27	8.1, 8.2.1
(1)	*139*
(2)	4.2
s 28	1.2.4, 5.2, *86, 152*
(1)	*86*
(3),(4)	5.6, *87*
s 29	5.8.2, 7.2, 7.6.6, *89, 90*
s 30	1.2.5, 5.3, 6.1, 6.3, 6.5.1, 7.5.1, *94, 101*
s 31	*110*
(4)	*110*
s 32	3.7.2, *110*
s 34	1.2.4, *110*
(1)	1.2.1
s 36	1.2.4, 4.7, *110*
(1)	*139*

Law of Property Act 1925 *cont*
  s 36(2)   1.2.1
    (7)   4.7
  s 53(1)(b)   3.2, *106, 107*
  s 130(1),(3)   *107*
    (6)   *107*
  s 205   *101*
    (xxi)   8.1
    (xxix)   1.2.4
  Sch 1   *111*
Law of Property (Joint Tenants) Act
1964   1.2.5, 8.5.2

Matrimonial and Family
Proceedings Act 1984
  s 3   6.5.1
Matrimonial Homes Act 1983   7.5.1
Mental Health Act 1983   4.3.1
  Pt VII   2.2.13, 4.6

Partnership Act 1890
  s 22   *103*
Pensions Act 1995   5.7.1
  s 35(4)   *88*
Powers of Attorney Act 1971   5.8.2
  s 4   5.8.2, *89*
  s 5   8.4, *89*
  s 9   5.8.1
    (2)   1.2.5, 5.2
Public Trustee Act 1906   4.2

Rent Act 1977   7.5.1
Reverter of Sites Act 1925   *85*
Reverter of Sites Act 1987   5.7.5, 7.5.1
  s 1   5.7.5, *111*

Settled Land Act 1925   1.1, 1.2.1, 1.2.2,
     1.2.3, 1.2.7, 1.4.3, 2.2.2, 3.3.1,
     3.3.2, 3.3.3, 3.3.4, 3.3.7, 3.3.8,
     3.5, 3.7, 3.7.1, 3.8.1, 5.2, 6.3,
     7.2, 7.4, 8.5.2, *84, 97, 102, 137*
  s 1   1.2.2, 2.2.2
    (1)(v)   3.3.3, *107*
  s 4   1.2.3
  s 17   1.2.5, 8.5.1
  s 18   1.2.2, 8.2.1
  s 23   1.2.2
  s 26   1.2.2
  s 27   *106*
    (1)   3.3.2

s 29   1.2.2, *107*
  (1)   *90*
s 30(1)(v)   4.5
s 36(4)   1.2.1
s 64   6.3
s 72   1.2.2
s 75(2)   *155*
s 106   1.2.4, 7.2, *88, 155*
s 107   1.2.3
s 110   8.2.1
  (5)   1.2.5, 1.2.7, 8.5.1
Settled Land Act 1929
  s 73(2)   *86*
Statutory Instruments Act 1946
  s 5(1)   *103*
Supreme Court Act 1981
  s 116   1.2.3

Trustee Act 1925   4.4, 5.8.1, 6.3, *86, 102*
  s 19   5.2, *86, 94*
  ss 20, 21   *94*
  s 23   5.8.1, *89, 90*
  s 25   5.8.1, 5.8.2, *89, 90*
    (2)   1.2.5, 5.2
  s 31   4.6
  s 34   5.4, *99*
    (2)   4.2
  s 36   *100*
    (1)   4.3.1
      (a)   4.4
      (b)   4.4, *98*
    (6)   4.3.2, 4.4
      (b)   *98*
    (7)   *100*
  s 37   4.4
  s 40(1)(b)   *151*
    (2)   *99*
    (3)   *99*
  s 41   4.4
  s 57   6.3
Trustee Investment Act 1961   5.7.4, *86,*
     87
Trusts of Land and Appointment of
  Trustees Act 1996   1.2.1, 1.3, 1.4.4, 2.1,
     2.2.1, 2.2.2, 2.2.3, 2.2.4, 3.2,
     3.3.5, 3.6, 3.7.1, 3.7.3, 3.7.4,
     3.8.1, 4.3, 5.7.1, 5.8.1, 5.8.2,
     5.9, 5.10.2, 6.6, 7.2, 7.3, 7.4,
     7.5.1, 7.8, 8.1, *139, 140, 142,*
     144, 145

Trusts of Land and Appointment of		s 11(1)	2.2.8, 5.7.5, 8.3.2, *137*
Trustees Act 1996 *cont*		(a)	*137*
Pt I	2.2.12	(b)	*137*
s 1	2.1, 7.9	(2)	*137*
(1)	2.2.1	(a)	2.2.8, 5.7.5, 7.6.4, 7.10.1
(a)	3.1, 6.2	(b)	2.2.8, 5.7.5, 7.6.4
(2)	2.2.1, 3.1, 8.2.2	(c)	2.2.8, 5.4, 5.7.5, 7.6.4
(3)	2.2.1, 3.1, 3.2, 3.4	(3)	2.1, 2.2.8, 5.7.5, 7.6.4, *135,*
s 2	2.1, 2.2.2, 4.3.3, 8.6		*137, 144*
(1)	3.3.1, 3.3.6	(b)	*144*
(2)	2.2.2, 3.3.8	(4)	2.2.8, 5.7.5
(3)	2.2.2, 3.3.8, 3.8.1, *137*	s 12	7.3, 7.5.1, 7.10.1
(4)	2.2.2, 3.3.7	(1)	2.2.9, *137*
(5)	2.2.2, 3.3.4	(2)	2.2.9, 7.5.1
(6)	3.3.2, 3.3.3, 3.3.4, 3.3.5, 7.5.1	s 13	6.5.2, 7.5.1
s 3	7.4, *152*	(1)	2.2.9, 7.5.1, *138, 154*
(1)–(3)	2.2.3	(2)	*154*
s 4	3.6	(2)–(8)	2.2.9, 7.5.1
(1)	2.2.4, 5.3, *136*	(6)	*138, 154*
(3)	2.2.4	s 14	5.6, 6.1, 6.4, 7.9
s 5	2.2.5, 3.7	(1)	2.2.10, 6.2
s 6	5.2, *137, 152*	(2)	2.2.10, 6.3
(1)	2.2.6, 5.1, 7.5.1	(a)	6.3
(2)	2.2.6, 5.4, 7.8, *135, 137, 139*	(3)	2.2.10, 6.4, 7.9
(3),(4)	2.2.6, 5.5	(4)	6.3
(5)	2.2.6, 5.7.3, 7.6.2, 8.3.1	s 15	5.3, 6.1, 6.5.1
(6)	2.2.6, 5.1, 5.7.4	(1)	2.2.10, 7.9
(7),(8)	2.2.6, 5.7.4	(2)	2.2.10, 6.5.2, 7.9
s 7	*152*	(3)	2.2.10, 5.4, 6.5.3, 7.9
(1)	2.2.6, 5.6, *137*	(4)	2.2.10, 6.6
(2)	2.2.6, 5.6, *135*	s 16(1)	2.2.11, 5.6, 8.1, 8.3.1, 8.3.2,
(3)	2.2.6, 5.6, 7.6.3, 8.3.3, *137, 141*		8.3.3
(4)	5.6	(2)	2.2.11, 8.1
(5)	2.2.6, 5.6	(3)	2.2.11, 5.7.1, 7.6.5, 8.1, 8.3.4,
s 8	5.2, 8.3.4		8.3.5
(1)	2.2.6, 5.7.1, 7.10.1, *137*	(4)	2.2.11, *135, 139, 140, 145*
(2)	2.2.6, 5.1, 5.7.1, 7.6.3, 7.10.1, *137*	(5)	2.2.11, 8.1, 8.5.3, *139*
(3),(4)	2.2.6, 5.7.1	(6)	2.2.11
s 9	5.8.2, 7.3, 7.6.6	s 17(1)	2.2.6, 5.5
(1)	2.2.6, 7.6.6, 8.4, *135, 138, 142, 143,*	(2)	2.2.10, 6.2, 7.9
	155	s 18(1)–(3)	2.2.12, 5.9
(2)	2.2.6, 8.1, 8.4, *135, 143*	s 19	4.1, 4.4, 7.3, *146, 150, 151*
(3),(4)	2.2.6, 5.8.2, *142*	(1)	2.2.13, 7.7
(5)	2.2.6, *142*	(2)	2.2.13, 4.5, *135, 138*
(6)	2.2.6, 5.8.2	(a)	*146, 148, 151*
(7)	2.2.6, 5.8.2, 7.6.6, *142*	(b)	*146, 148*
(8),(9)	2.2.6, 5.8.2	(3)	2.2.13, 4.7, *135, 148*
s 10	7.6.3	(b)–(d)	*148*
(1)	2.2.7, 8.3.3	(4)	2.2.13, 4.7, *149*
(2)	2.2.7	(5)	2.2.13
(3)	2.2.7	s 20	*146, 150, 151*
(a)	8.3.3	(1)	2.2.13, 4.6
(b)	7.6.3, 8.3.3	(2)	2.2.13, *135, 147*
s 11	5.1, 7.6.4	s 21(1)	4.9, *135, 146, 150*

Trusts of Land and Appointment of
  Trustees Act 1996 *cont*
  s 21(2)   4.9, *146*
       (3),(4)   4.9
       (5)   2.2.13, 4.1, 7.7, 7.10.1, *138*
       (6)   2.1, 2.2.13, 4.1, 7.7, 7.10.2, *135,
                                            137, 151*
       (7)   2.2.13, 4.1, *137, 151*
       (8)   2.2.13, 4.1, *137*
  s 22(1)   5.7.3, 7.1
       (2)   5.8.2, 7.1
       (3)   5.8.2, 7.1, 7.5.1, 7.6.6
  s 24   2.1
  s 25(1)   4.3.2, 6.6
       (3)   3.5
  s 26   2.1
  s 27(2), (3)   2.1
  Sch 1
       para 1   3.3.2
              (2)   4.3.3
       para 3   3.3.3
       para 4   3.3.4, 8.6

para 5   3.3.5
para 6   3.3.7
Sch 2   3.7
  para 1   3.7.1
  para 2   3.7.2
  paras 3, 4   3.7.4
  para 5   3.7.3, 3.8.2
Sch 3
  para 4   8.1, 8.2.2
       (11)   4.3.2
  para 5(8)   8.2.2, 8.3.4
            (c)   2.2.11
  para 6(2)   7.5.1
       (4)   3.3.5
       (6)   7.5.1
  para 12   7.4
  para 23   2.2.10, 6.6

Universities and College Estates Act
  1925   2.2.1, 3.1, 3.2, 3.4, *83*

TABLE OF STATUTORY INSTRUMENTS

References are to paragraph numbers except where they are in *italics* which are references to page numbers.

High Court and County Court Jurisdiction Order 1991, SI 1991/724
  art 2, para 1(a)   *101*

GLOSSARY

1996 Act	References to the 1996 Act are to the Trusts of Land and Appointment of Trustees Act 1996
Absolute owner	An owner who holds the property for himself absolutely, not in a fiduciary capacity.
Attorney	
power of	Authority to another person to carry out transactions and execute deeds.
enduring power of	A power of attorney under the Enduring Powers of Attorney Act 1985 which will not be revoked by the donor's subsequent mental incapacity.
Beneficiary	Any person with an interest in trust property including trustee and personal representative. [1996 Act, s 22(1)]
Beneficiary who is entitled to an interest in possession of land	A person defined above with an interest giving him a present right to present enjoyment but excluding an annuitant. Possession includes receipts of rent and profits or the right to receive the same if any. [LPA 1925, s 205(1)(xix)]
Beneficiary who is beneficially entitled	Any person with an interest in the trust property other than an interest as trustee or personal representative only. [1996 Act, s 22(2)]
Charitable trust	A public trust for charitable purposes.
Charity commissioners	Persons empowered by statute to supervise charities.
Conversion, doctrine of	A notional change in character of the property.
Court	High Court or county court. [1996 Act, s 23(2)]
Direction	Written instructions by beneficiaries to trustees, re appointment and retirement of trustees.

Disposition	Document
Ecclesiastical trust	Charitable trust for Church purposes.
Full age and capacity	At least 18 years old and not subject to the Court of Protection.
Good faith	An act carried out honestly.
Incumbrance	Includes a legal or equitable mortgage and a trust for securing money, and a lien and a charge of a portion, annuity or other capital or annual sum. [LPA 1925, s 205(1)(vii)]
Intestacy	Dying without leaving a will.
Minor	Person under 18 years old.
Overreaching	The transfer of rights from an interest in land to purchase money.
Personal property	Goods and chattels.
Personal representative	The executor, original or by representation or administrator for the time being of a deceased person. [LPA 1925, s 205(1)(xviii)]
Public trust	Trusts for charitable or non-charitable public purposes.
Purchaser	A person who acquires an interest in or charge on property for money or money's worth. [1996 Act, s 23(1); LPA 1925, s 205(1)(xxi)]
Relevant property	For purposes of s 2(4) of the 1996 Act, land subject to settlement under the SLA 1925 heirlooms to which s 67(1) of the SLA 1925 applies.
Settlement	Instrument making provisions for persons in succession.
Severalty	Each share is ascertained.
Statutory declaration	Written statement of facts signed before appropriate person, eg solicitor under Statutory Declarations Act 1835.
Strict settlement	Settlement governed by the SLA 1925.
Trust	A bare, constructive, express, implied, resulting trust for sale. [1996 Act, ss 1(2), 17(4)]

bare	Property held by trustee as nominee for beneficiary.
constructive	A trust imposed by equity.
express	Expressly declared by creator of the trust.
implied	Imposed by statute.
resulting	Trust where property reverts to grantor.
trust for sale	Trust with duty to sell.
Trust corporation	Public trustee or corporation appointed by the court.
Trustees of sale	The persons (including a personal representative) holding land on trust for sale. [LPA 1925, s 205(1)(xxix)]
Trust for sale	An immediate binding trust for sale, whether or not exercisable at the request or with the consent of any person. [LPA 1925, s 205(1)(xxix)]
Trust of land	Any trust of property which consists of or includes land. [1996 Act, s 1(1)(a)]
Trustees of land	Trustees of a trust of land. [1996 Act, s 1(1)(b)]
Trust of proceeds	Any proceeds of a disposition of land held in trust including settled land and any property representing such proceeds but not the proceeds of a trust which remains a settlement for the purposes of SLA 1925. [1996 Act, s 17(4), (5)]
Undivided shares	The interest of a tenant in common.

Chapter 1

THE NEED FOR LEGISLATION

1.1 INTRODUCTION

In 1989, the Law Commission as part of its programme for simplification of conveyancing made recommendations for the reform of the law relating to trusts of land. In its report, it stated:

> 'We consider that the present dual system of trusts for sale and strict settlements is unnecessarily complex, ill-suited to the conditions of modern property ownership, and liable to give rise to unforeseen conveyancing complications. We propose that it should be replaced by an entirely new system, applicable to all trusts of land except existing Settled Land Act settlements, set out in broader and simpler provisions designed to resolve existing difficulties whilst continuing to provide security for beneficiaries and purchasers alike.'[1]

1.2 THE DUAL SYSTEM

1.2.1 Successive and concurrent interests in land

Before the commencement of the Trusts of Land and Appointment of Trustees Act 1996, it was possible to create successive or concurrent interests in the same piece of land by means of the strict settlement or trust for sale.

An example of a successive interest is where land is left to a spouse for life with remainder to a child. An example of a concurrent interest is where land is conveyed to a husband and wife jointly. A gift to a spouse for life with a remainder to the children equally would be a successive and a concurrent interest.

Concurrent interests generally exist behind a trust for sale. The main exception is where land is settled under the Settled Land Act 1925 on two or more people as tenant for life.[2]

1.2.2 Strict settlements

The strict settlement is the older form of settlement. It was used to keep land within the family by granting a series of interests such as a life interest, followed by an entailed interest with an ultimate remainder. Legislation in

---

1. The Law Commission (Law Com No 181) Transfer of Land Trusts of Land 8 June 1989 HMSO p iv. See also Law Com WP No 94 October 1985.
2. Since 1925, the legal estate must be held by joint tenants. It cannot be held as tenants in common. Law of Property Act 1925, ss 1(6), 34(1) and 36(2); Settled Land Act 1925, s 36(4).

the mid-nineteenth century made the management and alienation of land subject to a strict settlement much easier.

The Settled Land Act 1925 governs the current law relating to strict settlements. The legal estate is vested in the tenant for life,[3] or where there is none, the statutory owners.[4] The tenant for life has the power of sale and control of the management of the property. On the sale of the property, provided capital money is paid to at least two trustees, the beneficial interests are transferred from the land to the proceeds of sale.[5] Although the interests of the beneficiaries are protected in this way because the powers of the tenant for life, including the power of sale, cannot be fettered, it is not possible to ensure that the actual property is kept within the family.

Land was settled not only where it was expressly limited in trust for any persons by way of succession. It was also settled where the land was conveyed to an infant or the estate was liable to be determined on the happening of a certain event, or where it was subject to a family charge.[6] Land held on charitable, ecclesiastical or public trusts was deemed to be settled land.[7]

1.2.3   Problems with strict settlements

Strict settlements could be complex. In order to create a valid strict settlement, two documents are necessary, the trust instrument which sets out the trusts and the vesting deed which vests the property in the tenant for life or statutory owner.[8] If land is acquired subsequently, a subsidiary vesting deed will be necessary. On the death of the tenant for life where the settlement continues, the land does not devolve with the rest of the estate of the deceased. Instead, it vests in the special personal representatives who are the trustees of the settlement.[9] It is they who must vest the legal estate in the person next entitled.

Strict settlements may be created inadvertently where, say, a person makes a gift to 'A' for life. The donor would not have considered appointing trustees and there are complex provisions in the Settled Land Act 1925 for ascertaining who should be the trustees. Inadvertent strict settlements may also arise where a person is given the right to live in a property for his lifetime.

The Law Commission Report[10] quotes from its Working Paper, para 16.16 (omitting the footnotes):

---

3. Settled Land Act 1925, s 4.
4. Eg Settled Land Act 1925, ss 23, 26.
5. Settled Land Act 1925, ss 72, 18.
6. Settled Land Act 1925, s 1.
7. Settled Land Act 1925, s 29.
8. Settled Land Act 1925, s 4.
9. Administration of Estates Act 1925, s 22. Supreme Court Act 1981, s 116.
10. Law Com No 181.

'*Inadvertent settlements.* Inadvertent settlements fall into two categories. The first are those where the intention is to create some sort of trust or settlement, and the settlor, by failing expressly to subject the land to a trust for sale, brings it within the Settled Land Act 1925. If, as is likely, this is a trust in a will, the executors may not realise the true effect of the provisions and the wrong procedure may be followed, causing problems for subsequent purchasers .... The second type of inadvertent settlement occurs when a person is given the right to reside in a property during his lifetime, and subject to that right the property is conveyed or passes on death to another. At present the result of such an arrangement may be that the land is settled land under the Settled Land Act 1925, and the person with the right of residence is the tenant for life with full powers of disposition and management. This result may be thought to be unsatisfactory, as there was no intention to confer such an extensive interest on the tenant for life. However, these cases should not necessarily be seen as wrongly decided. As Megarry and Wade put it, "it has to be remembered that the deliberate policy of the Act is that the statutory powers must always be available, so that the land is not sterilised, and that these powers cannot be restricted or fettered, whatever the settlor's intentions. This policy may naturally produce unintended results, but that is not necessarily a good reason for excluding a case from the purview of the Act."'

Another problem is that the tenant for life has the legal estate which he holds as trustee for the benefit of all the beneficiaries under the trust and his own beneficial interests.[11] There is therefore a potential conflict of interest. The courts have sometimes allowed the tenant for life to exercise his powers to the detriment of the remainderman.[12]

1.2.4 Trusts for sale

The trust for sale was not initially for the purpose of keeping land within the family. It was used where it was intended that the land should be sold, perhaps where the proceeds were to be split between the children, or where the land had been bought as an investment.

The legal estate is vested in the trustees who hold the land on behalf of the beneficiaries. The beneficiaries' interests may be either successive or concurrent.[13]

---

11. Settled Land Act 1925, s 107.
12. *Re Thornhill's Settlement* [1941] Ch 24. *England v Public Trustee* (1968) 112 SJ 70 *Re Pennant's Will Trust* [1970] Ch 75.
13. Law of Property Act 1925, s 28. The trustees have all the powers of the tenant for life and trustees under a strict settlement.

The Law of Property Act 1925 defines a trust for sale as an immediate binding trust for sale, whether or not exercisable at the request of or with the consent of any person and with or without a power to postpone the sale.[14]

It is therefore possible for the land to be held and not sold. Also, because the person setting up the trust can stipulate that the consents of specified persons are necessary before a sale can take place it became a better means of keeping the land in the family. As has been explained, a tenant for life's powers under a strict settlement cannot be fettered.[15]

Trusts for sale also arose where there were concurrent interests in property. These might have been expressly created or have arisen by operation of law. The Law of Property Act 1925 imposed a trust for sale where property was conveyed to more than one person either as joint tenants or as tenants in common.[16] The transferees hold the legal estate on trust for themselves.

A trust for sale was also implied where land was conveyed to one person, but two or more persons contributed to the purchase price.[17]

1.2.5   Problems with trusts for sale

As the Law of Property Act 1925 imposes a trust for sale whenever land is conveyed to co-owners, or where land is conveyed to one owner, but the other has an equitable interest, many co-owners of houses find themselves holding the property on trust for sale. To the layman, this is a surprising result. Owners who have just purchased a house do not generally intend to sell. In 1925, when the legislation was passed, ownership of the freehold of dwellinghouses was not the norm and it would have been unusual for the property to be purchased in joint names.

In the words of Lord Mishcon on the Second Reading in the House of Lords:[18]

> 'As the Law Commission report points out, house ownership is a common feature today among all sections of our community. The figures are interesting. The proportion of owner-occupied dwellings goes from 7 per cent in 1914 to 43 per cent in 1938 and 77 per cent by

---

14. Law of Property Act 1925, s 205(xxix). For a criticism of this definition, see Megarry and Wade *The Law of Real Property* 5th edn (Sweet & Maxwell) pp 386–388. Meaning of binding is uncertain. *Re Parker's Settled Estates* [1928] Ch 247; *Re Ryder and Steadman's Contract* [1927] 2 Ch 62; *Re Norton* [1929] 1 Ch 84; *Re Beaumont Settled Estates* [1937] 2 All ER 353; *Re Sharpe's Deed of Release* [1939] Ch 51.
15. Settled Land Act 1925, s 106.
16. Law of Property Act 1925, ss 34, 36.
17. This is not expressly covered by the legislation. See Megarry and Wade *The Law of Real Property* 5th edn (Sweet & Maxwell) pp 437–438. *Bull v Bull* [1955] 1 QB 234.
18. Hansard Vol 569 No 1657 col 1722.

1992. In the old days joint ownership on the title deeds by husband and wife was a rarity. In these days it is very common, and the intention of most spouses when purchasing the matrimonial home in joint names is not to hold it as an investment for sale or as an investment pending sale but to use it and keep it as a home. Lawyers have been trying to deal with the position by developing a principle, to which the noble and learned Lord briefly referred, known as "collateral purpose". That means recognising that the intention and purpose was to provide a family home so that where there is a dispute the court can refuse to order a sale. In many respects, that has made confusion more confounded in regard to what is the true legal position and, as has been pointed out, there are conflicting precedents in the judgments of the Court of Appeal.'

Not only is co-owned property held on trust for sale, but even before the sale the interests of the beneficiaries are deemed to be in the proceeds of sale and not in the land itself. The doctrine of conversion developed in the eighteenth century because the law of inheritance differed for real and personal property. In order that the beneficiaries' future should not depend on whether the trustees had got round to selling or not 'equity looked on that as done that which ought to be done' and treated the land as money from the outset. Today the law of inheritance on intestacy is the same for real and personal property. The doctrine of conversion is 'just a little unreal'[19] and the courts' application of the doctrine has been inconsistent.[20]

Under the previous law where trustees refused to exercise their powers or where the necessary consents to the exercise of those powers could not be obtained, any person interested could apply to the court for an order to give effect to the transaction.[21] However, it was not clear who could apply under the section, the extent of the powers of the court and what the court had to take into account in reaching its decision.

Another problem was whether the beneficiaries under a trust for sale had a right of occupation.[22] Generally, the beneficiaries were in a weak position as far as control was concerned. Beneficiaries of a trust of land are in the same position as beneficiaries of other kinds of property. However, as the trust may consist of the beneficiaries' home, questions of control are important.

---

19. *Williams & Glyn's Bank Ltd v Boland* [1981] AC 487, 507 per Lord Wilberforce.
20. *Re Kempthorne* [1930] 1 Ch 208; *Barclay v Barclay* [1970] 2 QB 677; *Irani Finance v Singh* [1971] Ch 59. Cf *National Westminster Bank v Allen* [1971] 1 QB 718; *Williams & Glyn's Bank v Boland* [1980] 2 All ER 408; *Elias v Mitchell* [1972] Ch 632; *Bull v Bull* [1955] 1 QB 234; *Jones v Jones* [1977] 1 WLR 438; *Cooper v Critchley* [1955] Ch 431; *Cedar Holdings Ltd v Green and Another* [1979] 3 All ER 117.
21. Law of Property Act 1925, s 30.
22. *Barclay v Barclay* [1970] 2 QB 677 (no right of residence in express trust for sale). *Bull v Bull* [1955] 1 QB 234 (right of residence where statutory trust for sale).

Trustees have limited powers. Technically, they cannot raise the initial purchase price for a house by mortgage.[23] In theory, this could cause problems where co-owners purchased a property. In practice, as they are usually beneficiaries as well, no problems occurred. Nor could a co-owner appoint his co-trustee as an attorney.[24] A third person had to be appointed and a special trustee form of attorney used.

One major drawback from the conveyancer's point of view is that unless he inspected the equitable title, he had no means of knowing that a trust for sale had terminated. He therefore had to insist on a second trustee being appointed to ensure that the equitable interests were overreached. There was no equivalent of the deed of discharge and statutory provision which enables a purchaser to assume that a strict settlement has come to an end.[25]

1.2.6　Problems with the dual system

It is unsatisfactory to have two systems for trusts of successive interests, especially when most of the advantages of the strict settlement could be achieved by the trust for sale.

It was often difficult to decide at the outset whether a strict settlement or trust for sale had been created.[26] There could also be problems in deciding when a strict settlement ended and a trust for sale arose. This had important consequences for a purchaser. If it were a strict settlement, he would only obtain good title from the tenant for life, not the trustees.

Moreover, priority was given to strict settlements. In order for there to be a trust for sale, words had to be used which indicated that there was an immediate binding trust for sale. If not, and the property was simply left in trust or for successive interests, a strict settlement would result. This was not always appreciated where property was left by will, especially in a home-made will. Land which should have been vested in the tenant for life might have been vested by the executors in trustees or in the beneficiary absolutely. This could cause complications on sale.[27]

---

23. See *Emmett on Title*, para 10.140.
24. Trustee Act 1925, s 25(2) as substituted by Powers of Attorney Act 1971, s 9(2).
25. Settled Land Act 1925, ss 17, 110(5). Limited protection is given to a purchaser under Law of Property (Joint Tenants) Act 1964 where conveyance by surviving joint tenant.
26. *Re Herklots Wills Trust* [1964] 1 WLR 585; *Re Leigh's SE (No 1)* [1926] Ch 852.
27. *Re Duce and Boots Cash Chemists (Southern) Ltd's Contract* [1937] Ch 642.

1.2.7 Comparison chart showing differences between strict settlements and trusts for sale

Settlements Settled Land Act 1925	Trusts for sale Law of Property Act 1925
1 Legal estate in tenant for life or statutory owners.	1 Legal estate vested in trustees.
2 Tenant for life's powers cannot be fettered.	2 Trustees' powers of sale may be subject to consents of specified persons.
3 Favours one beneficiary, the tenant for life.	3 Beneficiaries can be provided for equally.
4 Advantages: – Control is given to the tenant for life. – Deed of discharge and presumption of s 110(5) protects a purchaser when settlement at an end.	4 Disadvantages: – Beneficiaries do not have control. The power of sale cannot be delegated. – Purchaser must always insist on two trustees being appointed or investigate the equitable interests to discover if the vendor is absolutely entitled when a trust for sale ends.
5 Disadvantages: – Expensive and complex; 2 documents needed to set up settlement. – Special grants of probate needed on death of tenant for life when settlement continues. – Conflict of interest.	5 Advantages: – Cheaper and simpler. – No change of legal ownership on death of beneficiary. – Advantages of strict settlement can be obtained for trust for sale – (i) power to postpone sale (ii) power to delegate leasing and management. Additional advantages: (i) trusts for sale can dispose of a person's entire estate, stocks, shares, money etc. as well as land. (ii) it is a better way of keeping property in the family. The settlor may specify that the consent of beneficiaries should be obtained before a sale. Alternatively the court might find there was a collateral purpose of the trust and thus not order a sale.

1.3 BARE TRUSTS

A bare trust arises where the entire beneficial interest is vested in one person but the legal estate is in another. The real owner is the beneficiary who can direct the trustee. The trustee has no duties other than to obey instructions. In other words, the property is vested in a nominee.

Before the 1996 Act, bare trusts were outside the statutory provisions relating to strict settlements and trusts for sale. This could cause inconvenience, in particular as the overreaching provisions did not apply.

1.4 BACKGROUND TO THE REFORM

1.4.1 The Law Commission Working Paper on trusts of land

In 1985, the Law Commission published a Working Paper (Law Com No 94) criticising the law relating to trusts of land. It suggested five separate options for reform:

(1) the abolition of the dual system of strict settlements and trusts for sale and its replacement with a new trust of land. All trusts for sale and strict settlements would be converted into trusts of land;

(2) the prohibition of new strict settlements and the conversion of all existing settlements into settlements under a trust for sale;

(3) a reversal of the rule that a strict settlement would be created unless there were clear words indicating a trust for sale. This would prevent a strict settlement being created inadvertently;

(4) a new form of co-ownership not involving a trust for sale where the legal and equitable interests are identical;

(5) minor changes to correct some of the difficulties which have been already outlined.

1.4.2 The response

The majority of respondents favoured option (1). Some respondents, however, argued that there was a need to preserve the strict settlement. The advantage of the strict settlement over the trust for sale was that control was given to the tenant for life. This could be important where there was a capable surviving spouse who might not want to be subject to the dictates of trustees. There was also concern about converting existing settlements into a trust of land.

1.4.3 The Law Commission Report on trusts of land

On 8 June 1989, the Law Commission Report on Transfer of Land Trusts of Land (Law Com No 181) was published with the draft Bill annexed. It took into account the responses to the Working Paper by recommending that strict settlements should remain in existence and subject to the Settled Land Act 1925, but that it should be impossible to create new strict settlements or to add new land to existing settlements.

The Law Commission considered that the benefits of simplified trusts of land outweighed the advantage of retaining the strict settlement, especially as strict settlements were so rarely expressly created. Instead, it suggested that the main advantages of a strict settlement, namely the ability to give control, including the power of sale to the life tenant, could be achieved by the trustees delegating their functions.

1.4.4   The Law Commission Report on overreaching

On 19 December 1989, the Law Commission published its report, Transfer of Land – Overreaching Beneficiaries in Occupation (Law Com No 188). It recommended that the interest of a beneficiary under a trust who was of full age and capacity and who was occupying trust property with a right to do so, should not be overreached unless he consented. It also recommended that the beneficial interests under a bare trust should be overreached on a sale.

This second recommendation has been given effect to in the 1996 Act as bare trusts are treated in the same way as other trusts of land.

1.4.5   Lord Chancellor's Department

The Lord Chancellor's Department made changes to the scheme having taken into account views expressed by other departments and government organisations, including the Crown Estate, the Land Registry and the Charity Commission, as well as professional bodies such as the Law Society and the General Council of the Bar.

It made changes in the proposals relating to strict settlements, introduced transitional provisions in respect of the trustees' duty to consult beneficiaries and the position of personal representatives of a person dying before the commencement of the legislation and gave extra protection to beneficiaries where title to land is registered. The actual Bill was redrafted so as to make it more user friendly and free standing, rather than relying heavily on textual amendment of existing legislation.

1.4.6   Parliamentary passage

During the passage of the Bill through the Houses of Parliament, several important changes were made. The most fundamental change was to allow beneficiaries to give directions not only as to the appointment, but also on the retirement of trustees. Hansard references are given in Appendix II.

Chapter 2

APPLICATION AND OUTLINE OF THE TRUSTS OF LAND AND APPOINTMENT OF TRUSTEES ACT 1996

2.1 APPLICATION

The Act which received Royal Assent on 24 July 1996 applies to trusts of land in England and Wales.[1] It binds the Crown.[2]

The statute will come into force on the date specified by the Lord Chancellor in a statutory instrument.[3] The Lord Chancellor is given power to make consequential provisions in existing public, general or local Acts.[4]

Some of the provisions apply to trusts created or arising before the commencement of the Act.[5] Other provisions apply to trusts created or arising after that date.[6] There are also provisions which will apply to existing trusts if a subsequent deed so allows[7] and ones which will not apply if a subsequent deed disallows.[8]

2.2 OUTLINE

2.2.1 Meaning of trust of land

Trust of land means any trust of property which consists of or includes land.[9] The term covers trusts created or arising before, as well as after, the commencement of the Act. The trust may be an express, implied, resulting or constructive trust.[10]

Trusts for sale and bare trusts come within the definition. However, existing strict settlements and derivative settlements are excluded. Also excluded is land to which the Universities and College Estates Act 1925 applies.[11]

---

1. Trusts of Land and Appointment of Trustees Act 1996, s 27(3).
2. Ibid, s 24.
3. Ibid, s 27(2).
4. Ibid, s 26.
5. Eg ibid, s 1.
6. Eg ibid, s 2.
7. Ibid, s 11(3).
8. Ibid, s 21(6).
9. Ibid, s 1(1).
10. Ibid, s 1(2).
11. Ibid, s 1(3).

2.2.2 Strict settlements

The general rule is that it will not be possible to create a strict settlement after the commencement of the Act, either expressly or by virtue of s 1 of the Settled Land Act 1925.[12]

However, existing strict settlements will continue as such. Moreover, a resettlement of a strict settlement will remain a strict settlement, as will resettlements of resettlements. A strict settlement can also be created where there is an exercise of a power of appointment contained in settlements in existence at the date of the commencement of the Act.[13]

It is possible for the instruments creating the new trusts on a resettlement or the exercise of a power of appointment to specify that the new trust is not to be a strict settlement.[14]

If there is a strict settlement existing at the commencement of the Act but there is no longer any land or heirlooms to which the Settled Land Act 1925 applies then it will cease to be a strict settlement.[15]

Land which is held on charitable, ecclesiastical or public trusts will not be or deemed to be settled land after the commencement of the Act even if the trust arose before that date.[16]

2.2.3 Abolition of the doctrine of conversion

The doctrine whereby land held under a trust for sale is deemed to be an interest in personal property even before the sale is abolished. Reverse conversion whereby interests in money or personal property are deemed to be an interest in land is also abolished.[17] The doctrine will no longer apply to any trust whether it is created or arises before or after the commencement of the Act[18] except to a trust created by the will of a testator who died before the commencement of the Act.[19]

2.2.4 Express trusts for sale

There is implied into every trust for sale, whether it is created or arises before or after the commencement of the Act, a power to postpone the sale. This is notwithstanding any provision to the contrary in the disposition. The trustees in exercising their discretion, can postpone the sale for an

---

12. Ibid, s 2.
13. Ibid, s 2(2).
14. Ibid, s 2(3).
15. Ibid, s 2(4).
16. Ibid, s 2(5).
17. Ibid, s 3(1).
18. Ibid, s 3(3).
19. Ibid, s 3(2).

indefinite period without incurring liability.[20] However, they are not exonerated from any liability incurred before the commencement of the Act.[21]

2.2.5   Implied trusts for sale

Where there were statutory provisions which gave rise to an implied trust for sale, there will now instead be a trust of land without a duty to sell.[22]

2.2.6   Functions of the trustees

The trustees for the purpose of exercising their functions have all the powers of an absolute owner.[23]

Where the beneficiaries are of full age and capacity and absolutely entitled the trustees have power to convey the land to the beneficiaries even where the beneficiaries have not requested them to do so. The beneficiaries must do anything necessary to vest the land in themselves and should they fail to do so the court can make an order to that effect.[24]

The trustees of land (and the trustees of a trust of the proceeds of sale of land) have power to purchase land by way of investment, for occupation by any beneficiary or for any other reason.[25]

However, the powers are subject to any order made under any other enactment or rule of law or equity.[26] The trustees must comply with any restriction, limitation or condition under such enactment.[27] They must also have regard to the rights of the beneficiaries.[28]

The trustees have power, where the beneficiaries are absolutely entitled as tenants in common to partition the land and convey it to the beneficiaries in accordance with that entitlement. The land may be conveyed absolutely or in trust and the trustees may provide for the payment of equality money. The beneficiaries must consent to any conveyance.[29]

Where the land is subject to an incumbrance, the trustees have a discretion whether to convey the property subject to it or provide for its discharge from the property allocated to that share.

---

20. Ibid, s 4(1).
21. Ibid, s 4(3).
22. Ibid, s 5.
23. Ibid, s 6(1).
24. Ibid, s 6(2).
25. Ibid, ss 6(3) and (4), 17(1).
26. Ibid, s 6(6).
27. Ibid, s 6(8).
28. Ibid, s 6(5).
29. Ibid, s 7(1), (2) and (3).

If a beneficiary is absolutely entitled but not of full age, the powers to partition still exist but the trustees may act on his behalf and retain the land or other property representing his share on his behalf.[30]

The disposition may exclude, or make subject to consents, the general powers of the trustees and their right to partition the land.[31] However, such exclusions or requirements will be ineffective if there is an enactment which overrides provisions to that effect in any disposition.[32] Dispositions cannot cut down the powers of trustees in charitable, ecclesiastical or public trusts.[33]

Trustees may delegate their functions to beneficiaries of full age who are beneficially entitled to an interest in possession to the trust land.[34] The delegation must be by power of attorney.

A third party dealing in good faith with the donee of a power can presume, unless the third party had at the time of the transaction actual knowledge to the contrary, that the donee is the beneficiary to whom the functions could be delegated.[35]

A subsequent purchaser can rely on a statutory declaration made by a third party before or within three months of the completion of the sale to the effect that he dealt in good faith and did not have such knowledge.[36]

A power of attorney must be given by all the trustees but may be revoked by any one of them. If a new trustee is appointed then the power will automatically be revoked. However, where there is no new appointment the death or retirement of a trustee will not cause the power of appointment to lapse.[37]

The general rule is that if the functions are delegated to a beneficiary and he ceases to be entitled to an interest in possession in the land subject to the trust the power is revoked. If the functions are delegated to him and other beneficiaries jointly and each of the beneficiaries ceases to be entitled to an interest then the power is revoked. However, if only one or some of the beneficiaries cease to be entitled, the functions continue to be exercisable by the remaining beneficiaries. If the functions are delegated to him

---

30. Ibid, s 7(5).
31. Ibid, s 8(1) and (2).
32. Ibid, s 8(4).
33. Ibid, s 8(3).
34. Ibid, s 9(1).
35. Ibid, s 9(2).
36. Ibid.
37. Ibid, s 9(3).

separately or separately and jointly, the power is revoked as far as he is concerned.[38]

A delegation may be made for any period of time or indefinitely.[39] However, the power of attorney cannot be an enduring power of attorney under the Enduring Powers of Attorney Act 1985.[40]

The trustees' liability is limited. Although they are liable both jointly and severally for any default of a beneficiary in exercising the functions this liability arises only if the trustees did not exercise reasonable care in deciding to delegate.[41]

Beneficiaries to whom the functions have been delegated have the same duties and liabilities as the trustees. For these purposes only they are in the same position as trustees. They are not, however, regarded as trustees for any other purpose. They cannot sub-delegate their functions nor can they receive capital monies so as to overreach the equitable interest of any beneficiary.[42]

Delegation before the commencement of the Act will be governed by the old rules.[43]

2.2.7   Consents

A trust instrument may require the consent of specified persons to the exercise of the functions of the trustees. Even if more than two consents are required a purchaser will only be concerned to ensure that two consents are obtained.[44]

These provisions do not apply to charitable, ecclesiastical or public trusts.[45]

If the consent is needed of a person who is not of full age, the purchaser need not require any consent. The trustees, however, must obtain the consent of his parents or guardians.[46]

2.2.8   Consultation

In exercising their functions, the trustees must, so far as practicable, consult the beneficiaries of full age who are beneficially entitled to an interest in possession and so far as is consistent with the general interest of the trust give

---

38. Ibid, s 9(4).
39. Ibid, s 9(5).
40. Ibid, s 9(6).
41. Ibid, s 9(8).
42. Ibid, s 9(7).
43. Ibid, s 9(9).
44. Ibid, s 10(1).
45. Ibid, s 10(2).
46. Ibid, s 10(3).

effect to their wishes. If there is a dispute, the wishes of the majority according to the value of their combined interests will prevail.[47]

A trust instrument can exclude the power to consult beneficiaries.[48]

There is no duty to consult beneficiaries where the trust is created or arises under a will made before the commencement of the Act.[49]

The power of the trustees to convey land to beneficiaries absolutely entitled can be exercised even against the wishes of the beneficiaries. There is therefore no duty to consult them.[50]

There are contracting-in provisions for trusts, other than those in wills, made before the commencement of the Act. A person who created a trust, provided he is of full capacity may by irrevocable deed state that the consultation provisions are to apply. Where the trust was created by more than one person all those who are alive and of full capacity must execute the deed.[51] Once executed the deed is irrevocable.[52]

2.2.9 Occupation by beneficiary

A beneficiary who is beneficially entitled to an interest in possession has a right to occupy the land if the purpose of the trust includes making land available for him or for a class of beneficiaries of which he is a member or if the trustees hold land which is available for that purpose.[53]

A beneficiary will not have a right to occupy land if it is unavailable or is unsuitable for occupation by him.[54]

If there are two or more beneficiaries with a right of occupation the trustees may decide who shall be entitled to occupy the land.[55] They must however not unreasonably exclude or restrict any entitlement to occupy the land.[56]

The trustees may from time to time impose reasonable conditions on a beneficiary's right to occupy land.[57] The conditions which trustees may impose include a condition requiring a beneficiary to pay any outgoings or expenses in respect of the land or to comply with obligations relating to the land or any activity conducted thereon.[58]

---

47. Ibid, s 11(1).
48. Ibid, s 11(2)(a).
49. Ibid, s 11(2)(b).
50. Ibid, s 11(2)(c).
51. Ibid, s 11(3).
52. Ibid, s 11(4).
53. Ibid, s 12(1).
54. Ibid, s 12(2).
55. Ibid, s 13(1).
56. Ibid, s 13(2).
57. Ibid, s 13(3).
58. Ibid, s 13(5).

Where a beneficiary occupies land and as a result the right of any other beneficiary has been excluded or restricted he may be required to pay compensation to such person or persons or to forgo any payments or other benefits under the trust so as to benefit that beneficiary.[59]

Trustees must not exercise their powers so as to prevent any person who is in occupation of land from continuing to occupy the land or in a manner likely to cause him to cease to occupy unless he or the court consents.[60]

In exercising their powers to exclude or restrict occupation the trustees must have regard to the intentions of the person who created the trust, the purpose for which the land is held and the circumstances and wishes of the beneficiaries who qualify for the right to occupy the land.[61]

In deciding whether or not to give approval where a beneficiary's continuing occupation is under threat, the court must have regard to the same considerations.[62]

2.2.10   Powers of the court

On an application by a trustee of land (or a trustee of the proceeds of sale of land) or by a person with an interest in the property subject to the trust, the court may make an order relating to the exercise by the trustees of any of their functions. Such an order can relieve the trustees of their need to obtain the consents of any person or to consult the beneficiaries. Orders can also be made declaring the nature or extent of a person's interest in the trust property.[63] The court cannot, however, make any order as to the appointment and removal of trustees.[64]

In determining an application the court has to pay regard to the intentions of the persons who created the trust, the purposes for which the trust property is held, the welfare of any minor who occupies or might expect to occupy the property as his home and the interests of any secured creditor of a beneficiary.[65] The court must also have regard to the circumstances and wishes of any beneficiary of full age who is entitled to an interest in possession in the trust property, or, where there is a dispute, the majority of the beneficiaries according to the value of their combined interest. Where there is a question of the trustees conveying land to beneficiaries who are absolutely entitled, their circumstances and wishes are irrelevant.[66]

---

59. Ibid, s 13(6).
60. Ibid, s 13(7).
61. Ibid, s 13(4).
62. Ibid, s 13(8).
63. Ibid, ss 14(1) and (2), 17(2).
64. Ibid, s 14(3).
65. Ibid, s 15(1).
66. Ibid, s 15(3).

Where the application to the court concerns the occupation of the land where two or more beneficiaries are entitled, the court has to take into account the circumstances and wishes of each beneficiary who is entitled to occupy the land.[67]

These provisions do not apply where an application is made by a trustee of a bankrupt. The Insolvency Act 1986 sets out the matters which have to be considered in such a situation.[68]

2.2.11   Protection of a purchaser

A purchaser is not concerned with whether or not the trustees have regarded the rights of the beneficiaries. Nor does he have to ensure that the consent of the beneficiaries has been obtained to any partition of the land or if they have been consulted before the trustees exercised any of their functions.[69]

A conveyance of trust land which is made in contravention of, or of any order made in pursuance of, any enactment or rule of law or equity, or of any restriction, limitation or condition imposed by any enactment will not invalidate the conveyance provided the purchaser has no actual knowledge of the contravention.[70]

If the trust instrument excludes or restricts the powers of the trustees such limitation will not invalidate the conveyance if the purchaser has no notice of the limitation. The trustees are, however, under a duty to take all reasonable steps to bring the limitation to the notice of any purchaser.[71]

A purchaser of trust land is entitled to rely on a deed of discharge executed by the trustees, after they have conveyed the former trust property to the beneficiaries, and assume that a trust has terminated unless he has actual knowledge that the trustees were mistaken in their belief that the beneficiaries were absolutely entitled to the land and were of full age and capacity.[72]

These provisions do not apply to charitable, ecclesiastical or public trusts.[73]

Where the land is registered the position of the purchaser will depend on whether there is any restriction or caution on the register. The Registrar can rely on a deed of discharge executed by the trustees unless he has actual knowledge that the beneficiaries were not absolutely entitled to the land or were not of full age and capacity.[74]

---

67. Ibid, s 15(2).
68. Ibid, s 15(4); Sch 3, para 23.
69. Ibid, s 16(1).
70. Ibid, s 16(2).
71. Ibid, s 16(3).
72. Ibid, s 16(4) and (5).
73. Ibid, s 16(6).
74. Ibid, Sch 3, para 5(8)(c).

2.2.12   Personal representatives

Most of the provisions in Part I of the Act apply to personal representatives as well as trustees. The exceptions are those sections dealing with consents and consultation and the powers of the court.[75]

In order for the sections to apply, the term 'persons interested in the due administration of the estate' has to be substituted for 'beneficiaries', and the term 'will' for 'disposition creating the trust'.[76]

If a person dies before the commencement of the Act the doctrine of conversion will continue to apply to property held by his personal representatives.[77]

2.2.13   Appointment and retirement of trustees

Provided there is no person nominated in the trust instrument for appointing new trustees, the beneficiaries who are of full age and capacity and together absolutely entitled to the trust property, can give written directions for the retirement or appointment of a trustee.[78] A trust instrument may exclude these powers. [79] Although the powers apply to trusts created before the commencement of the Act, the creator or creators of the trust can execute a subsequent deed excluding them.[80]

Protection is given to a trustee who is directed to retire. Where:

(1) reasonable arrangements have been made for the protection of any interest of his under the trust;
(2) after his retirement there will be either a trust corporation or at least two trustees remaining; and
(3) another person is to be appointed trustee in his place or the continuing trustees consent to his retirement,

the retiring trustee is under an obligation to execute a deed declaring his retirement. The effect of this is that he is deemed to have retired and will be discharged from the trust.[81] However, he has the ability to delay executing the deed until reasonable arrangements for his protection have been made.

Where a trustee retires, the continuing trustees and any new trustees must do whatever is necessary to vest the property in the continuing and new trustees.[82]

---

75. Ibid, s 18(1).
76. Ibid, s 18(2).
77. Ibid, s 18(3).
78. Ibid, s 19(1) and (2).
79. Ibid, s 21(5).
80. Ibid, s 21(6), (7) and (8).
81. Ibid, s 19(3).
82. Ibid, s 19(4).

No appointment of a new trustee can be made which would mean that the number of trustees exceeded four.[83]

There are special provisions where a trustee is incapable because of a mental disorder from exercising his functions as trustee. If there is no one nominated for the purpose of appointing new trustees by the trust instrument, or such a person is unwilling to act, and the surviving or continuing trustees or the personal representative of the last surviving or continuing trustee is unwilling to act, the beneficiaries may give written directions specifying a trustee or trustees to be appointed in place of the incapable trustee. As with the other provisions relating to directions, the beneficiaries must be of full age and capacity and taken together must be absolutely entitled to the trust property.[84]

The written directions must be given to a receiver of the trustee, or to an attorney under an instrument which has been registered under the Enduring Power of Attorney Act 1985 or a person authorised for the purpose by the authority having jurisdiction under Part VII of the Mental Health Act 1983.[85]

---

83. Ibid, s 19(5).
84. Ibid, s 20(1).
85. Ibid, s 20(2).

Chapter 3

TRUSTS OF LAND

3.1 MEANING OF TRUST OF LAND

A trust of land means any trust of property which consists of or includes land.[1] A mixed trust of land and personal property will be a trust of land. It includes an express, implied, resulting or constructive trust as well as what were, before the commencement of the Act, trusts for sale and bare trusts.[2] Excluded from the definition are strict settlements and land to which the Universities and College Estates Act 1925 apply.[3]

3.2 CREATION OF TRUST OF LAND

After the commencement of the Act, all new trusts relating to land will be trusts of land. It will no longer be possible to create a completely new strict settlement and any express trust for sale will be a trust of land with a power to postpone the sale. The trust of land will apply whether the trust is expressly created or statutorily implied. It will apply whenever there is a conveyance to co-owners. It will also apply wherever equitable interests in land arise by way of resulting, constructive or implied trusts. The trust of land will cover both concurrent and successive interests.

There are no special formalities for the creation of the trust, other than that the trust must be properly constituted in accordance with the general law.[4]

Existing strict settlements will continue as strict settlements but existing express and implied trusts for sale will be converted to trusts of land.

Land held under the Universities and College Estates Act 1925[5] will not be a trust of land. Such land has never been settled land but has its own detailed, self-contained scheme of land holding.

---

1. Trusts of Land and Appointment of Trustees Act 1996, s 1(1)(a).
2. Ibid, s 1(2).
3. Ibid, s 1(3).
4. Law of Property Act 1925, s 53(1)(b), a declaration of trust must be manifested and proved by writing.
5. Trusts of Land and Appointment of Trustees Act 1996, s 1(3).

3.3   STRICT SETTLEMENTS

3.3.1   General rule

Although existing settlements will continue, new strict settlements with certain exceptions are prohibited after the commencement of the Act.[6] This general rule applies not only to express strict settlements but also those which are deemed to be strict settlements under the Settled Land Act 1925. Examples of deemed strict settlements are where there is a conveyance to a minor or a charitable trust.[7]

3.3.2   Minors

Under the Law of Property Act 1925, a conveyance to a minor created a strict settlement. The Trusts of Land and Appointment of Trustees Act 1925[8] provides that where there is a purported conveyance to a minor or minors, the grantor will hold the land on trust for the minor or minors. If the conveyance is on trust for other persons, the grantor will hold the property on trust for those other persons. Conveyances to minors as joint tenants or as tenants in common are covered by the provision.

The conveyance, although ineffective to transfer the legal estate, operates as a declaration of trust and so complies with the requirement that a declaration of trust respecting any land, or interest therein, must be evidenced in writing.

Where the conveyance is to an adult or adults, together with a minor or minors, the adult or adults hold the land on trust for themselves as well as the minor or minors. If the conveyance is on trust for other persons, the adults will hold on trust for those other persons.

Under the Settled Land Act 1925,[9] any attempt to convey a legal estate in land to a minor or minors took effect as a specifically enforceable agreement to execute a strict settlement in favour of the minor or minors and in the meantime to hold the land on trust for them.

After the commencement of the Act, this is no longer the law. Moreover, any agreements which are subsisting at the commencement date will cease to have effect. The conveyance will subsequently operate instead as a declaration that the land is held on trust for the minors.

Where for any other reason, such as an intestacy, land would vest in a minor were he of full age, the land is held on trust for the minor.

---

6. Ibid, s 2(1).
7. Law of Property Act 1925, s 19.
8. Trusts of Land and Appointment of Trustees Act 1996, s 2(6) and Sch 1, para 1.
9. Settled Land Act 1925, s 27(1).

3.3.3 Family charges

Another example of a strict settlement being created under the Settled Land Act 1925 was where land was subject to a family charge.[10] Where land is charged in consideration of marriage or by way of family arrangement with a rentcharge for a person's life or some shorter period or with capital, annual or periodical sums for any person made by an instrument coming into operation after the commencement of the Act, it will take effect as a declaration that the land is held in trust for giving effect to the charge.[11] Normally the person who has the land subject to the charge will have the legal estate vested in him and he will hold it on trust to give effect to the charge. If he wants to sell the land he can either overreach the charge by appointing another trustee or sell the land subject to the charge.

3.3.4 Charitable, ecclesiastical and public trusts

Before the 1996 Act, all such trusts were deemed to be settled land for the purposes of s 29 of the Settled Land Act 1925. The instrument creating the trust was treated as the settlement and the trustees were deemed to be the trustees of the settlement and to have all the powers conferred by the Settled Land Act 1925 on the tenant for life and trustees of the settlement. The position now is that the land will be held under a trust of land, rather than a strict settlement, even if it was, or deemed to be, settled land before the commencement of the Act.[12]

At Report Stage in the House of Lords,[13] the Lord Chancellor explained the reasons as follows:

> 'The Bill presently draws no distinction between charitable trusts and what may be termed "private" settlements, where land is limited in succession for individuals. As the Bill is presently drafted, all settlements in existence at the time of commencement would remain untouched by the new regime and subject to the Settled Land Act for as long as they remain in existence as settlements. It has been cogently argued, however, that charities would benefit from the more flexible trustee powers conferred on trustees of land, and that while it would not be right to convert existing "private" settlements into trusts of land and change the position of the tenant for life, there is no such problem in the case of charitable trusts.'

The Charities Act 1993 provides, with some limited exceptions, that charity land may not be disposed of without an order of the court or the Charity Commissioners.[14] Any contract for the sale or for a lease or other

---

10. Ibid, s 1(1)(v).
11. Trusts of Land and Appointment of Trustees Act 1996, s 2(6) and Sch 1, para 3.
12. Ibid, s 2(5), (6) and Sch 1, para 4.
13. Hansard Vol 571 No 1664 cols 954, 955.
14. Charities Act 1993, s 36.

disposition of land which is held by or in trust for a charity, and any conveyance, transfer, lease or other instrument effecting a disposition of such land, has to state that it is so held. It must also state whether the charity is an exempt charity and whether it is a disposition to which the restrictions on dispositions do not apply.[15]

If the statements cannot be given, the instrument must state that the restrictions apply.

The charity trustees must certify in the instrument effecting the disposition that all the consents and requirements under the Charities Act 1993 have been complied with.

Where the title to land is registered there is a requirement, with limited exceptions, for an appropriate restriction to be entered on the register to prevent any disposition taking place which does not comply with restrictions on disposition of charitable land.

The Charities Act 1993 also lays down similar rules for mortgages held by or in trust for a charity.[16]

If there is a conveyance of land which is not covered by the relevant provisions in the Charities Act 1993 regarding the statements and certificates required to be given by the trustees, the conveyance must state that the land is held on charitable, ecclesiastical or public trusts. Any purchaser with notice that it is held on such trusts will have to see that any necessary consents or orders have been obtained.[17]

3.3.5   Entailed interests

After the commencement of the 1996 Act, it is no longer possible to grant to another person an entailed interest. All attempts to do so will operate as a declaration of a trust of land in favour of the grantee.[18] If a person purports to grant a freehold in tail, the intended tenant in tail in possession will be entitled to a fee simple in possession. Provided he is not a minor he can call for the trustees to transfer the legal estate to him as he will be absolutely entitled.

The instrument which purports to create the entailed interest will not pass any legal estate in the land. It operates as a declaration of trust.

The provision applies to an instrument which comes into operation after the Act, even if the instrument was executed before. It applies to both real and personal property.

---

15. Ibid, s 37.
16. Ibid, ss 38, 39.
17. Trusts of Land and Appointment of Trustees Act 1996, s 2(6) and Sch 1, para 4.
18. Ibid, s 2(6) and Sch 1, para 5. See also consequential amendments to s 51(3) of the Administration of Estates Act 1925 made by Sch 3, para 6(4).

If a person purports by an instrument coming into effect after the commencement of the Act to declare himself a tenant in tail of either real or personal property, the instrument is ineffective.

So if A purports to declare himself trustee in tail for B, he will simply remain the owner. If he purports to declare himself trustee for B for life and then to C in tail, B's life interest will be valid. On the death of B the property will revert to A or his estate.

3.3.6 Conditional and determinable fees

The Law of Property Act 1926[19] provides that a fee simple which is subject to a legal or equitable right of re-entry is a fee simple absolute and so therefore is a legal estate. That provision will continue. However, any determinable or conditional fee simple outside that provision will be a trust of land. The trustees will be the grantor or the personal representatives.[20]

3.3.7 Settlement ceasing to exist

A strict settlement ceases to be subject to the Settled Land Act 1925 when there is no longer any relevant land or heirlooms subject to the settlement.[21] Any land or settled chattels which subsequently becomes subject to the settlement is held on trust. If the trust includes land, then it will become a trust of land.

3.3.8 Exceptions to the general rule

As has been stated, no express or deemed strict settlements may be created after the commencement of the Act. However, new land may be brought into an existing settlement and it will still be governed by the Settled Land Act 1925.[22]

A resettlement of a strict settlement which is in existence at the commencement of the Act will continue to be a strict settlement and will not be a trust of land. For example, if there were a pre-1996 Act settlement whereby a settlor left land to A for life with remainder to B for life, then remainder to C for life and remainder in fee simple to D, and B and C resettle their life interests on

---

19. Law of Property Act 1925, s 7(1). The exact scope of this provision is uncertain. It may extend to all conditional fee simples. The distinction between determinable fees and conditional fees is artificial and has been called a disgrace to our jurisprudence.
20. Trusts of Land and Appointment of Trustees Act 1996, s 2(1).
21. Ibid, s 2(4) and Sch 1, para 6. Strict settlements will also cease to exist under the Settled Land Act 1925 where the limitations under the settlement cease or are incapable of being exercised or a minor reaches his majority.
22. Ibid, s 2(2).

E, with remainder to themselves as joint tenants, the resettlement, even if it takes place after the commencement of the Act, will continue to be a strict settlement under the Settled Land Act 1925. Resettlements of resettlements also come within the exceptions.

The exercise of a power of appointment which is contained in a strict settlement pre-dating the Act will take effect as a strict settlement. For example, if a settlement made in 1950 contains a power in favour of A to allocate land and any other property to any of B's grandchildren, for what interest and in what shares he thinks fit, and A exercises this power in 1998 by appointing the property to C for life, with remainder to D and then to E, the allocation will take effect as a strict settlement under the Settled Land Act 1925.

The reason for having these exceptions is to avoid confusion and management conflicts, were part of the land in a trust to be subject to a trust of land and part to a strict settlement. This is because the legal estate in a trust of land is vested in the trustees, whilst in a strict settlement it is vested in the tenant for life (or statutory owners). If the additional land were acquired to enhance the land in the original settlement and it was intended that in the future the land, or part of it, might be sold as a single parcel, there could be difficulty in co-ordinating the different holders of the legal estates. There could also be difficulties in other administration matters such as repairs, boundaries and use of land, in deciding who should take decisions and how the duty to consult beneficiaries would operate.

However, it is possible that the instrument creating the new trusts, which would otherwise count as strict settlements, may stipulate that the new trusts shall be a trust of land.[23]

3.4   UNIVERSITIES AND COLLEGE ESTATES ACT 1925

The Universities and College Estates Act 1925 applies to the Universities of Oxford, Cambridge and Durham, and to Winchester and Eton Colleges. Land held by those bodies will not be subject to a trust of land.[24]

3.5   THE CHEQUERS AND CHEVENING ESTATES

The settlements of the Chequers and Chevening estates, although not charitable, ecclesiastical or public trusts, are set out by statute. They are not therefore private trusts in the ordinary way. Nevertheless, they will continue to be governed by the Settled Land Act 1925.[25]

---

23. Ibid, s 2(3).
24. Ibid, s 1(3).
25. Ibid, s 25(3).

3.6   EXPRESS TRUSTS FOR SALE

In an express trust for sale of land, there is to be implied, despite any provision to the contrary, a power for the trustees to postpone the sale.[26] The trustees are not liable in any way for postponing the sale. However, this does not affect any liability incurred by the trustees before the commencement of the Act.

In the Law of Property Act 1925,[27] although there was an implied power to postpone the sale, this could be excluded where there was a contrary intention. Now even where there is a contrary intention, it will be overruled by the 1996 Act which applies to a trust whether it is created or arises before or after the Act.

3.7   STATUTORY TRUST FOR SALE

All implied trusts for sale at the commencement of the Act are converted into trusts of land without a duty to sell.[28] It will not be possible in future to create such trusts. The Settled Land Act 1925 does not apply to any land held on an implied trust for sale which now becomes a trust of land.

3.7.1   Mortgaged property where redemption barred

Where any property is vested in trustees and the property becomes by virtue of the statute of limitation or an order of foreclosure discharged from the right of redemption, instead of being held as formerly on trust for sale, a trust of land will be imposed.[29] The changes apply whether the right of redemption was discharged before or after the commencement of the Act but do not affect any dealings or arrangements made before the commencement.

The trustees under the trust must apply the income from the property in the same way as interest on the mortgage debt would have been applied. If the property is sold the net proceeds of sale, after payment of costs and expenses, have to be applied in the same manner as the mortgage debt would have been applied. However, this is without prejudice to any rule of law relating to the apportionment of capital and income between the tenant for life and remainderman.

---

26. Ibid, s 4.
27. Law of Property Act 1925, s 25. Although the power to postpone could be excluded by agreement the settlor may not have always realised this. See *Re Rooke* [1953] Ch 716; *Re Atkins' Will Trusts* [1974] 1 WLR 761.
28. Trusts of Land and Appointment of Trustees Act 1996, s 5 and Sch 2.
29. Ibid, Sch 2, para 1.

There are special rules where new land is added to a settlement existing when the 1996 Act came into force. Where the mortgage money is capital money for the purposes of the Settled Land Act 1925, and the land is not part of a trust of land, the trustees of the strict settlement must execute a vesting deed in favour of a tenant for life or statutory owner, if required by him to do so.

3.7.2   Land purchased by trustees of personal property

Section 32 of the Law of Property Act 1925 provided that where a settlement of personal property or of land held upon trust for sale contained a power to invest in the purchase of land, such land would, unless the settlement provided otherwise, be held by trustees on trust for sale.

This section is now repealed in respect of land purchased after the commencement of the Act whether the trust or will, pursuant to which the land was purchased, came into operation before or after the Act came into force.[30]

3.7.3   Intestacy

Under the previous law, where a person died intestate all his property, both real and personal, was held on trust for sale.[31] Where a person died having made a will there was no automatic trust for sale although generally an express trust for sale, is created by the will. Those entitled under the will or intestacy are not strictly beneficiaries. They do not have an equitable interest while the property is still vested in the personal representatives. Their right is to see that the estate is properly administered.

After the commencement of the Act, whether the death occurs before or after, any real or personal estate of the intestate will be held in trust by his personal representatives with power to sell.[32]

3.7.4   Co-ownership

It was generally considered that all forms of co-ownership, other than where there were joint tenants for life under a strict settlement, held the property on trust for sale.[33] Under the 1996 Act, the trustees will hold the property on a trust of land whether the beneficial owners are tenants in common or joint tenants.[34] As there will be no duty to sell, this will accord with the realities of modern home ownership.

---

30. Ibid, Sch 2, para 2.
31. Administration of Estates Act 1925, s 33.
32. Trusts of Land and Appointment of Trustees Act 1996, s 5 and Sch 2, para 5.
33. See, however, Megarry and Wade *The Law of Real Property* 5th edn (Sweet & Maxwell) p 438.
34. Trusts of Land and Appointment of Trustees Act 1996, s 5 and Sch 2, paras 3 and 4.

3.8 POINTS FOR PRACTITIONERS

3.8.1 Derivative strict settlements

Where there are likely to be no management conflicts between the tenant for life and trustees, it might be sensible to provide, in instruments making new trusts in relation to existing strict settlements, that the new trust should be governed by the 1996 Act rather than the Settled Land Act 1925.[35] (See the clause in Precedent 12 in Appendix III for opting out of the Settled Land Act 1925.)

3.8.2 Gifts of residue by will

It is usual to provide that the testator's assets not otherwise disposed of will be held on trust for sale with power to postpone sale. This ensures that a strict settlement is not created where there are trusts for persons in succession, contingent interests or trusts for minors. Under the new law the residue can simply be left on trust.[36]

3.8.3 Express trust for sale

The advantage of having an express trust for sale is that there is a duty to sell, even though there is, notwithstanding any provision to the contrary, a power to postpone the sale. The difference between a duty and a power is that a power requires the trustees to be unanimous, whilst one trustee can insist on the performance of a duty.[37] If there are merely two powers, a power to sell and a power to postpone and there is a dispute, there are no rules on which to resolve the matter. It is likely that an application would then have to be made to the court. If, however, there is a duty to sell, this will override the power. The parties will know where they are and court costs may be avoided. It may therefore be advisable to include a duty to sell in conveyances to co-owners as one will not be implied by statute. (See Precedent 12.1.)

---

35. Ie advantage taken of s 2(3).
36. For intestacies, see Trusts of Land and Appointment of Trustees Act 1996, Sch 2, para 5.
37. *Re Mayo* [1943] Ch 302.

Chapter 4

APPOINTMENT AND RETIREMENT OF TRUSTEES

4.1 INTRODUCTION

In order for the section relating to the appointment and retirement of trustees to apply, two conditions must be satisfied. First, there must be no person who is still alive nominated for the purpose of appointing new trustees by the trust instrument. Secondly, all the beneficiaries must be of full age and capacity and together absolutely entitled to the trust property.[1]

The words 'together absolutely entitled' were added at Committee Stage in the House of Lords to make it clear that beneficiaries under a discretionary trust would not be able to give directions.[2]

In order to protect a purchaser the actual appointment is made by the existing trustees following the direction of the beneficiaries. This avoids the need for the purchaser to inquire into the details of the trust to establish whether he is dealing with properly appointed trustees.

The power of the beneficiaries to direct the appointment and retirement of trustees may be excluded by the disposition creating the trust.[3]

The new rules apply to a trust created before the commencement of the Act unless there is a deed, which provides that the rules shall not apply.[4] The deed must be executed by the person, being of full capacity, who created the trust. Where the trust was created by more than one person the deed must be executed by such of the persons as are alive and of full capacity.

The deed once executed is irrevocable.[5] It does not affect anything done before its execution to comply with directions, given by the beneficiaries. Where, however, the directions have been given but not complied with, the directions will cease to have effect.[6]

As there are no time-limits for executing the deed this may be done at any time. In practice, the person who created the trust may only consider executing a deed when the beneficiaries have given what he considers to be unsuitable directions.

The rules apply to trusts of personal property as well as trusts of land.

---

1. Trusts of Land and Appointment of Trustees Act 1996, s 19.
2. Hansard Vol 570 No 1661 col 1544.
3. Trusts of Land and Appointment of Trustees Act 1996, s 21(5).
4. Ibid, s 21(6).
5. Ibid, s 21(7).
6. Ibid, s 21(8).

4.2 APPOINTMENT OF INITIAL TRUSTEES

The original trustees are generally appointed in the will or settlement. If a settlor fails to appoint trustees, the property will revert to the settlor as trustee. If a testator fails to appoint trustees or they predecease him, the property will be held by the personal representatives. In both cases the property will be held on the terms of the trust.

Generally, any person who has the capacity to hold property can be a trustee. A minor cannot be appointed as a trustee, nor can he hold a legal estate.[7]

A corporation can be a trustee. Some corporations are known as trust corporations. These include the Public Trustee, the Treasury Solicitor, the Official Solicitor, certain charitable or public corporations and those corporations entitled to act as a custodian trustee under the Public Trustee Act 1906.

In a trust of land made after 1925 the maximum permitted number of trustees is four.[8] A minimum of two trustees are required to give a valid receipt, except where the trust is a trust corporation.[9]

In a trust of personal property, one trustee can give a receipt for capital money and there is no limit on the number of trustees who can be appointed.

There is a general equitable principle that 'equity does not want for a trustee'. This means that if a settlor has failed to appoint trustees, or if the appointed trustees refuse, or are unable to act or have ceased to exist, then the trust will not fail. There is an exception to this rule if the trust is conditional upon certain people acting as trustees.

4.3 APPOINTMENT OF SUBSEQUENT TRUSTEES

The settlor cannot appoint new trustees once the trust has been properly constituted unless there is an express power for him to do so. Although beneficiaries who are *sui juris* and entitled to the whole beneficial interest can terminate the trust under the rule in *Saunders v Vautier*,[10] it seems that before the coming into effect of the 1996 Act, beneficiaries could not appoint a new trustee. In *Re Brockbank*[11] the existing trustees were in disagreement with all the beneficiaries about whom should be appointed a new trustee. The beneficiaries and retiring trustee applied to the court. The

---

7. Law of Property Act 1925, s 20.
8. Trustee Act 1925, s 34(2).
9. Law of Property Act 1925, s 27(2).
10. (1841) 4 Beav 115.
11. [1948] Ch 206.

court held that the decision of the trustees should prevail over the wishes of the beneficiaries.

It is cumbersome and may have adverse taxation consequences for beneficiaries to have to end and reconstitute a trust for the sole purpose of controlling the appointment of trustees. The 1996 Act reverses the effect of *Re Brockbank* and entitles the beneficiaries to appoint new trustees except where the power to appoint trustees is vested in someone nominated for the purpose in the trust instrument.

The trust instrument may confer an express power of appointment. Reliance, however, is usually placed on the wide statutory power. The trust instrument will often nominate those who should exercise that power.

4.3.1 Replacement trustees

Unless there is a contrary provision in the trust instrument, the Trustee Act 1925[12] provides that a *replacement* trustee may be appointed where:

(a) the trustee is dead, including a person appointed in a will who dies before the testator;
(b) the trustee remains outside the United Kingdom for a continuous period exceeding 12 months. (This ground is often expressly excluded where for tax reasons all the trust property is outside the United Kingdom);
(c) the trustee wants to retire;
(d) the trustee refuses to act or disclaims before accepting office;
(e) the trustee is unfit to act, eg where he is bankrupt;
(f) the trustee is incapable of acting. This includes physical and mental illness (covered by the Mental Health Act 1983), old age and, in the case of a corporation, dissolution;
(g) the trustee of an implied resulting or constructive trust is an infant; or
(h) the trustee is removed under a power in the trust instrument.

4.3.2 Additional trustees

An additional trustee may be appointed in any case where there are not more than three existing trustees.[13]

4.3.3 Appointment of minors as trustees

A purported conveyance to a minor or minors, whether as joint tenants or tenants in common is ineffective. The conveyance takes effect as a declaration of trust. Where the conveyance is made inter vivos the grantor

---

12. Trustee Act 1925, s 36(1).
13. Ibid, s 36(6). Trusts of Land and Appointment of Trustees Act 1996, s 25(1) and Sch 3, para 3(11).

will hold the land as trustee for the minors. Where the disposition is testamentary, the personal representatives of the settlor will act as trustees. Where land is conveyed to a minor jointly with an adult, the adult will hold the land on trust for himself and the minor.

If, after the commencement of the Act, a legal estate would on an intestacy vest in a minor were he of full age, the land will be held on trust for him.[14]

4.4   WHO MAY MAKE THE APPOINTMENT?

An appointment made under the Trustee Act 1925 must be made in writing and should be made by:

(a) the persons nominated in the trust instrument for the purpose of appointing new trustees or failing such a person;[15]

(b) the beneficiaries who are of full age and capacity and together are absolutely entitled to the trust property.[16] The rules are explained below;

(c) if the beneficiaries do not exercise their rights, the surviving or continuing trustees.[17] The continuing trustees include those who are retiring or refusing to act, but not those being removed against their will;

(d) if such trustees are dead, then the personal representatives of the last surviving or continuing trustee.[18] This of course has no application where an additional trustee is being appointed;

(e) the court under the Trustee Act 1925.[19]

Where a trustee is being replaced, anyone can be appointed a new trustee including the appointor himself. He cannot, however, appoint himself when an additional trustee is being appointed.[20]

In trusts of both real and personal property it does not matter if the number of trustees is increased by the appointment, provided the number does not exceed four. Nor is there any need to fill up the numbers of trustees where they exceed two. In trusts of personal property where only one trustee was originally appointed there is no obligation to appoint more than one trustee and a trustee may be discharged leaving only one trustee. In other cases, there must be left either two or more trustees or a trust corporation to perform the trust.[21]

---

14. Ibid, s 2 and Sch 1, para 1(2).
15. Trustee Act 1925, s 36(1)(a).
16. Trusts of Land and Appointment of Trustees Act 1996, s 19.
17. Trustee Act 1925, s 36(1)(b).
18. Ibid.
19. Ibid, s 41.
20. Ibid, s 36(6).
21. Ibid, s 37.

4.5   DIRECTION BY THE BENEFICIARIES TO APPOINT TRUSTEES

The beneficiaries have power to give a written direction to a trustee or trustees for the time being, including anyone being directed to retire at the same time, to appoint as a trustee or trustees the person or persons specified in the direction. If there are no trustees then the direction has to be given to the personal representative of the last person who was a trustee.[22]

The power can be exercised only where there is no person nominated for the purpose of appointing new trustees by the trust instrument. In addition, the beneficiaries must be of full age and capacity and taken together absolutely entitled to the trust property.

4.6   DIRECTION FOR REPLACEMENT TRUSTEE

Where a new trustee is needed because of the mental disorder of an existing trustee, and there is no one entitled and willing and able to appoint a trustee in place of him under s 31 of the Trustee Act 1925, the beneficiaries may give the written direction to a receiver of the trustee, an attorney with an enduring power or a person authorised by the authority having jurisdiction under Part VII of the Mental Health Act 1983.[23]

Section 31 of the Trustee Act 1925 provides that the following may appoint new trustees:

(a) the person or persons nominated for the purpose of appointing new trustees by the instrument, if any, creating the trusts;
(b) if there is no such person, or no such person able and willing to act, then the surviving or continuing trustees or trustee for the time being, or the personal representatives of the last surviving or continuing trustees.

The recipient must appoint in writing the person or persons specified in the direction to be a trustee or trustees in place of the incapable trustee. More than one trustee may be necessary where the sole remaining trustee is unable to appoint a new trustee.

4.7   DIRECTION FOR THE RETIREMENT OF A TRUSTEE

The Bill, as originally drafted, did not contain a power for the beneficiaries to direct the retirement of a trustee. Lord Mishcon, at Committee Stage,

---

22. Trusts of Land and Appointment of Trustees Act 1996, s 19(2). Cf s 30(1)(v) of the Settled Land Act 1925 and *Re Spearman SE* [1906] 2 Ch 502.
23. Ibid, s 20(1).

suggested that the Bill should be amended to allow this.[24] As with all directions, the beneficiaries must be unanimous, of full age and capacity and between them entitled to the whole beneficial interest and there must be no person alive at the time of the direction nominated in the trust instrument for appointing new trustees.

The conditions for the retirement of a trustee are:

(a) a written direction must be given to him;
(b) reasonable arrangements must be made for the protection of any rights of his in connection with the trust;
(c) on his retirement there must remain a trust corporation or at least two trustees;
(d) a new trustee must be appointed on his retirement or, if no such appointment is to be made, the continuing trustees must consent by deed to his retirement;
(e) the retiring trustee must execute a deed of discharge (he has the ability to defer executing the deed until reasonable arrangements for his protection have been made);[25]
(f) the retiring and continuing trustees and any new trustee must do anything necessary to vest the trust property in the continuing and new trustees.[26]

4.8   PROTECTION OF A RETIRING TRUSTEE

A trustee who is directed to retire may have rights in respect of the trust property. He might have rights of reimbursement or indemnity for expenses incurred in relation to the trust and he may need to take action to ensure that he can enforce those rights. He may need to guard himself against taxation liabilities for which he could be held responsible after his retirement or he may have incurred contractual liabilities to third parties in dealing with the trust property.

The Act therefore provides that he shall only be under an obligation to execute a deed of retirement after reasonable arrangements have been made for the protection of any rights of his in connection with the trust.

---

24. Hansard Vol 570 No 1661 cols 1545–1547.
25. Trusts of Land and Appointment of Trustees Act 1996, s 19(3). As the appointment is not made under s 36 of the Law of Property Act 1925, there has to be a specific reference to s 36(7).
26. Trusts of Land and Appointment of Trustees Act 1996, s 19(4).

4.9 RULES ON DIRECTIONS

A direction can be given jointly by all of the beneficiaries or by each of them separately or by some of them separately and some of them jointly.[27] However, where more than one direction is given, each must specify for an appointment or retirement the same person or persons.[28]

A beneficiary may withdraw in writing a direction which has been given provided that it has not been complied with.[29] This power exists whether the direction was given jointly or singly. The purpose of the section is to deal with the risk of undue influence. At Committee Stage in the House of Lords, Lord Mishcon said:[30]

> 'An example could be where there is one dominant beneficiary, who perhaps by misrepresenting the history, induces the others – perhaps his children who have recently come of age – to sign a direction requiring the resignation of a trustee and perhaps the replacement of that trustee by the dominant beneficiary himself, when the trustee has in fact been resolutely standing up for their interests against the unreasonable demands of the dominant beneficiary.'

The trustee appointed will have the same powers as if he had been appointed a trustee by the instrument creating the trust.[31]

Directions for the appointment of new trustees of land and of new trustees of the proceeds of sale of land must specify the same persons for both. If there are already trustees of any trust of the proceeds of sale of the land, the directions must specify for appointment the same trustees for the land.[32]

4.10 POINTS FOR PRACTITIONERS

4.10.1 Written directions

Those acting for beneficiaries must serve directions on the trustees. (See Precedent 7 in Appendix III.) If it is inconvenient or would cause delay for a collective direction to be served, the beneficiaries can give separate directions. However, the directions must all specify the same person or persons to be appointed.

---

27. Ibid, s 21(1).
28. Ibid, s 21(2).
29. Ibid, s 21(1).
30. Hansard Vol 570 No 1661 col 1549.
31. Trusts of Land and Appointment of Trustees Act 1996, s 21(3).
32. Ibid, s 21(4).

4.10.2 Memorandum

Where new trustees of land are appointed, a memorandum of the persons who are for the time being trustees of the land must be endorsed or annexed to the conveyance by which the land was vested in the trustees.

4.10.3 Exclusion for new trusts

If the person who creates the trust does not want the beneficiaries to be able to direct the appointment or retirement of the trustees, this must be stated in the trust instrument. (See clause for excluding/restricting appointment provisions in Precedent 12.6 in Appendix III.)

4.10.4 Exclusion for existing trusts

If the person or persons who created the trust do not want the beneficiaries to be able to direct the appointment or retirement of trustees, he or they may execute a deed excluding the power. There is no time-limit on this opt-out provision. (See Precedent 11 in Appendix III.)

Chapter 5

POWERS OF TRUSTEES

5.1 INTRODUCTION

The Act gives more flexible management powers to the trustees but this is balanced by the extra rights of the beneficiaries. Trustees generally must consult the beneficiaries about the administration of the trust unless the creator of the trust has expressly provided to the contrary.[1] They must also comply with any provisions of other statues relating to trustees' powers[2] and must act in accordance with the general rules under trust law relating to trustees[3] and with the particular terms of the trust instrument.[4]

5.2 POWERS OF AN ABSOLUTE OWNER

Under the existing law, trustees for sale have all the powers of a tenant for life and the trustees of a settlement under the Settled Land Act 1925.[5] However, these combined powers fall short of the powers of an absolute owner.

For instance, trustees cannot raise the initial purchase price for a property by a mortgage.[6] This may not matter in practice because co-owners as beneficiaries are unlikely to object and mortgagees seldom do so.

There are also problems where one trustee wants to appoint the other as his or her attorney. This is not possible under the existing law[7] and so a third party has to be appointed.

In practice, many trust instruments have given wider powers to the trustees.

The statutory extension of the power is subject to the overriding principle that the trustees must act in a trustee-like manner. They must act in accordance with their general equitable duties and must not commit a breach of trust. The trustees are also subject to any restrictions relating to trustees' powers in any other statutes and to any specific limitations in the trust instrument.[8]

---

1. Trusts of Land and Appointment of Trustees Act 1996, s 11.
2. Ibid, s 6(6).
3. Ibid, s 6(1) and (6).
4. Ibid, s 8(2).
5. Law of Property Act 1925, s 28.
6. *Emmet on Title*, para 10.140.
7. Powers of Attorney Act 1971, s 9(2) replacing Trustee Act 1925, s 25(2).
8. Trusts of Land and Appointment of Trustees Act 1996, ss 6, 8.

Because trustees are given the powers of absolute owner, the provisions in various statutes which refer back to the Settled Land Act 1925 rules on payment of expenditure out of capital or income are repealed in so far as they would have been applicable to trusts for sale.[9]

Under s 19 of the Trustee Act 1925, trustees have a limited power to insure:

> 'A trustee may insure against loss or damage by fire any building or other insurable property to any amount, including the amount of any insurance already on foot, not exceeding three fourth parts of the full value of the building or property.'

Now that trustees have the power of absolute owners they can insure up to the full amount. Section 19 has therefore been amended so that it refers to personal property only.

5.3   POWER TO SELL OR RETAIN LAND

One of the major incidents of absolute ownership is that the owners can decide whether to sell or retain the property which they own.

Where there was concurrent ownership and either an express or statutory trust for sale, there was a duty to sell. This was because of the historical understanding that land held under a trust for sale was an investment.

As a consequence of the duty to sell, one trustee could force a sale even against the wishes of the others.[10] The power to retain, as for other powers, required unanimity.

The courts, to mitigate the effect of the duty to sell, have sought to find a collateral purpose of the trust. If it can, for example, find that the purpose of the trust is to provide a matrimonial home,[11] run a business at particular premises[12] or protect an open space,[13] the court will refuse to order a sale. Under the new law, where there is no duty to sell, the courts will be able to take a more flexible approach to the exercise of their powers.[14]

Where there was a conflict between the rights of the spouses or the secured creditors, the courts tended to favour the creditor.[15] The position of

9. Eg Landlord and Tenant Act 1927, s 13. Hill Farming Act 1946, s 11(2). Coast Protection Act 1949, s 11(2). Landlord and Tenant Act 1954, Sch 2, para 6. Agricultural Tenancies Act 1995, s 33.
10. *Re Mayo* [1943] Ch 302.
11. *Jones v Challenger* [1961] 1 QB 176.
12. *Bedson v Bedson* [1965] 2 QB 66.
13. *Re Buchanon – Wollaston's Conveyance* [1939] Ch 738.
14. Trusts of Land and Appointment of Trustees Act 1996, s 15. The matters to which the court has to pay regard are similar to those matters the court considered in applications under the LPA 1925, s 30.
15. Eg *Re Holliday* [1980] 3 All ER 385; *Re Lowrie* [1981] 3 All ER 353.

secured creditors is now dealt with specifically under the Insolvency Act 1986.[16]

It will still be open for a person who creates a trust of land to impose a duty to sell on the trustees. However, he will not be able to exclude the statutory power to postpone the sale.[17]

There may be good reasons for imposing a duty to sell to resolve any conflicts between the trustees, which might arise where some want to sell and others do not, without recourse to the court (see para **3.8.3**).

5.4 POWER TO CONVEY LAND TO A BENEFICIARY

Where each of the beneficiaries is of full age and capacity and absolutely entitled to land held under a trust of land, the trustees may convey the land to them whether or not the beneficiaries have requested them to do so.[18] The word 'each' means that the beneficiaries must have concurrent interests either as joint tenants or tenants in common. It does not cover the situation where there are successive interests. The trustees may exercise the power where one particular parcel of land is held for the beneficiaries absolutely, regardless of their interests in other land or assets of the trust.

Section 34 of the Trustee Act 1925 will apply to any such conveyance. This limits the number of trustees in whom the legal estate can be vested to four. A conveyance to more than four persons operates as a conveyance to the first four named in trust for all of them.

The purpose of the power is to enable trustees to bring the trust to an end where its continuation is unnecessary and for the trustees to be discharged from the trust.

Because this power is exercisable whether or not the beneficiaries so require, they do not have to be consulted.[19] Similarly, the court does not have to take into account the wishes of the beneficiaries when making an order.[20]

Where the trustees convey the land to the beneficiaries in pursuance of this section, the beneficiaries are under a duty to do whatever is necessary to secure that the property is vested in them. If they do not comply with this duty, the trustees may apply to the court for an order that they should do so.[21]

---

16. Insolvency Act 1986, s 355A.
17. Trusts of Land and Appointment of Trustees Act 1996, s 4(1).
18. Ibid, s 6(2). For a form of conveyance, see Precedent 1 in Appendix III.
19. Ibid, s 11(2)(c).
20. Ibid, s 15(3).
21. Ibid, s 6(2).

If, for instance, the title is registered, the beneficiaries are under a duty to apply to the Land Registry so that they may be registered and thus obtain the legal estate.

5.5   POWER TO PURCHASE LAND

Trustees of land and trustees of the proceeds of land have power to purchase land in England and Wales.[22] The power does not extend to purchasing land in other countries but the trust instrument could authorise the purchase of foreign land. This is the position under strict settlements and was formerly the position where there was a trust for sale.

However, the courts have interpreted the power to apply trust money in the purchase of land restrictively. In *Re Power's Will Trust*,[23] it was held that although trustees were expressly given all the powers of investment of an absolute owner, they could not purchase land for the occupation by the beneficiaries. It has also been held that where all the trust land had been sold the trustees ceased to be trustees for sale and therefore ceased to be within the statutory provisions.[24]

The Act specifically gives the trustees of land and trustees of the proceeds of sale of land, power to purchase land for occupation by the beneficiaries. They may also purchase land as an investment or for any other reason which is consistent with the trustees' general duties under the trust.[25]

The power extends to the purchase of both freehold and leasehold interests. There is no requirement that the lease has more than 60 years to run.

The Law Commission explained its thinking in the following terms:[26]

'. . . we felt that such a restriction was neither necessary nor desirable in today's economic climate, in which shorter leases may often be regarded as good and prudent investments, appropriate to the particular circumstances of the trust and the beneficiaries. The fixing of a minimum period, of whatever length, could only be the result of an arbitrary decision and, bearing in mind that there are circumstances in which it is quite conceivable that even a freehold might represent an imprudent or inappropriate investment, it seemed sensible to give trustees maximum flexibility, leaving general equitable rules to govern the use of such flexibility. In addition, the powers of trustees of land to mortgage, lease or sell the land should be analogous to those held by

---

22. Ibid, ss 6(3), 17(1).
23. [1947] Ch 572.
24. *Re Wakeman* [1945] Ch 177, cf *Re Wellstead's Will Trusts* [1949] Ch 296.
25. Trusts of Land and Appointment of Trustees Act 1996, ss 6(4), 17(1).
26. Law Com No 181 p 19 para 10.8.

absolute owners. Any money realised by the exercise of these powers will be held upon the same trusts as the land is or was held.'

5.6 POWER TO PARTITION

The Act gives the trustees power to partition the land into separate ascertained shares where the beneficial interest is in undivided shares, ie undivided shares in the whole.[27] It is an alternative to sale of the land and diversion of the proceeds. The trustees are empowered to make the necessary monetary adjustments between the beneficiaries if the property allotted to the shares is not of equal value.

Before the power can be exercised the beneficiaries must be of full age and absolutely entitled in undivided shares. In other words, the power only exists where the trust could be terminated.

The power is similar to that given to trustees under the Law of Property Act 1925.[28]

The land has to be conveyed to the beneficiaries in the ascertained shares according to their entitlement. This ends the co-ownership. After partition, there is separate ownership of the individual parcels of land, rather than co-ownership of the whole. The shares may be conveyed absolutely or in trust and may be conveyed subject to a mortgage created for raising equality money.[29]

The trustees must obtain the consent of the beneficiaries before conveying the land to them.[30] A subsequent purchaser from the beneficiary is not concerned to see that the consent was obtained.[31] An application may be made to the court by a trustee or person interested in the trust property to dispense with the need for consent.[32]

If the land is subject to an incumbrance the trustees may either give effect to this incumbrance in partitioning the land or provide for the incumbrance to be discharged from the property allotted to that share.[33]

There are special provisions where the share in the land is vested in a minor. The minor is treated as if he were of full age except that the trustees may act on his behalf and retain land or other property representing his share and hold it on trust for him.[34]

---

27. Trusts of Land and Appointment of Trustees Act 1996, s 7(1).
28. Law of Property Act 1925, s 28(3) and (4).
29. Trusts of Land and Appointment of Trustees Act 1996, s 7(2).
30. Ibid, s 7(3).
31. Ibid, s 16(1).
32. Ibid, s 14.
33. Ibid, s 7(4).
34. Ibid, s 7(5).

5.7   LIMITATIONS ON POWERS

Wide as the powers are, their exercise is not completely unfettered.

5.7.1   Trust instruments

The trustees must act in accordance with the trust instrument which may specifically restrict their powers.[35] Or it may make the exercise of the powers subject to consent of specified persons.[36]

However, a trust instrument cannot exclude or restrict the powers or make them subject to consents of trustees of a charitable, ecclesiastical or public trust.[37] Nor can it do so where there is any other enactment which prevents the exclusion or restriction of trustees' powers.[38]

For instance, the Pensions Act 1995 prevents the powers of trustees of occupational pension schemes being fettered by reference to any requirement to obtain the consent of the employer. The Trusts of Land and Appointment of Trustees Act 1996 prevents this requirement being unintentionally thwarted. Section 8(4) is drafted in general terms to ensure that similar provisions which may exist in other fields are not adversely affected.

Where the trustees' powers are validly excluded or restricted or made subject to consents, the trustees are under a duty to take all reasonable steps to bring any such limitation to the notice of a purchaser.[39]

5.7.2   General equitable duties

Although trustees are given by this statute the powers of an absolute owner, as trustees they have to act in the best interest of the trust even where this might conflict with their own personal code of honour.[40] In carrying out their powers the standard is the care a prudent man of business would exercise in managing his own affairs.[41] Trustees must not make a profit from their trust.[42]

In exercising powers the trustees must be unanimous.[43]

---

35. Ibid, s 8(1).
36. Ibid, s 8(2).
37. Ibid, s 8(3).
38. Ibid, s 8(4).
39. Ibid, s 16(3).
40. *Buttle v Saunders* [1950] 2 All ER 18.
41. *Speight v Gaunt* (1883) 9 App Cas 1.
42. *Keech v Sandford* (1726) Sel Cas t King 61.
43. *Luke v South Kensington Hotel Co* (1879) 11 Ch D 121, 125.

5.7.3 Regard to the rights of the beneficiaries

The trustees are expressly required in exercising the powers of an absolute owner, including the power of sale and purchase of land, to have regard to the rights of the beneficiaries.[44]

'Beneficiary' is defined to mean any person who under the trust has an interest in property subject to the trust including a person who has such an interest as a trustee or personal representative.[45]

5.7.4 Other enactments with restrictions

The powers of the trustees must not be exercised in contravention of, or any order made in pursuance of, any other enactment or any rule of law or equity. An order includes an order of any court or of the Charity Commissioners.[46]

Where trustees are given powers by other enactments which are subject to restrictions or limitations, trustees must comply with those provisions.[47] For instance, trustees must invest the proceeds of sale in accordance with the Trustee Investment Act 1961 unless greater powers are conferred in the trust instrument.

5.7.5 Consultation

Under the previous law there was no duty to consult beneficiaries unless in an express trust the trust instrument so provided or the trust for sale was implied by statute.[48]

The law is reversed for trusts of land. The trustees are under a duty so far as possible to consult the beneficiaries of full age and beneficially entitled to an interest in possession of land subject to the trust, and so far as consistent with the general interest of the trust to give effect to the wishes of those beneficiaries or a majority of them.[49] There is no duty to consult discretionary beneficiaries.

The duty does not arise if there is provision to the contrary in the trust instrument.[50]

Nor is there is a duty to consult where the trustees decide to convey the land to the beneficiaries, being of full age and capacity and together absolutely entitled to the land.[51] This is because the policy of the Act is to enable the

---

44. Trusts of Land and Appointment of Trustees Act 1996, s 6(5).
45. Ibid, s 22(1).
46. Ibid, s 6(6), (7).
47. Ibid, s 6(8).
48. Law of Property Act 1925, s 26(3).
49. Trusts of Land and Appointment of Trustees Act 1996, s 11(1).
50. Ibid, s 11(2)(a).
51. Ibid, s 11(2)(c).

trustees to discharge themselves from the trust, where it no longer serves any useful purpose, notwithstanding any views of the beneficiaries to the contrary.

There is no duty to consult beneficiaries if a trust is created by or arises under a will made before the commencement of the Act.[52] As a trust speaks from death the trust may not arise until after the commencement of the Act. Nevertheless, the testator may have assumed when making his will that the trustees would not have to consult the beneficiaries. Testators are unlikely to revise their wills because of changes in legislation.

The Lord Chancellor, at Report Stage,[53] explained the phrase 'created or arising under' as follows:

> 'The words "created or arising under" which are based on the precedent of paragraph 6 Schedule 3 to the Family Law Reform Act 1969, are intended to cover not only will trusts proper, but also trusts which may be created by assents by the personal representatives to beneficiaries under the will.
>
> The words "created or arising under" refer back to the time at which the original expression of the trust was made and the fact that there are later assents will not derogate from that.'

There are transitional provisions whereby creators of trusts existing at the commencement of the Act can opt into the consultation provisions.[54] The Law Commission's original recommendation was that the duty to consult should apply to all trusts of land whenever created unless expressly excluded or limited in the trust instrument. This was considered by the Lord Chancellor's Department likely to cause difficulties in relation to express trusts for sale in existence at the time of the commencement of the legislation. The person who created the trust might not have wanted the beneficiaries to be consulted and the requirement could impose unexpected burdens on the trustees. The Bill therefore provided that for such trusts there should be transitional provisions allowing settlors and beneficiaries to opt out of the requirement for consultation within a fixed period after the Act came into force.

At Committee Stage in the House of Lords, amendments were made so as to enable opting-in rather than opting-out. The Lord Chancellor said:[55]

> 'These provisions have been reconsidered in the light of representations from the legal profession, pointing out that a trust

---

52. Ibid, s 11(2)(b).
53. Hansard Vol 571 No 1664 cols 961, 962.
54. Trusts of Land and Appointment of Trustees Act 1996, s 11(3). See Precedent 5 in Appendix III.
55. Hansard Vol 570 No 1661 col 1541.

cannot be "opted out" if there is at commencement no settlor living and of full capacity. A settlor who has died or lost capacity might well have set up the trust in the knowledge that beneficiaries would not have the opportunity to control trustees' decisions in this way unless he spelt out the intention that they should have it; and it is therefore argued that the present transitional provisions will have the effect of changing the terms of some trust but not others on a capricious basis.'

The amendments mean that the consultation provisions will not apply to existing trusts, or new trusts created by reference to existing trusts, as where new land is added to an existing trust after the commencement of the Act, unless a deed is executed which states that the consultation provisions should apply. The deed once executed is irrevocable.[56] If the trust was created by one person that person being of full capacity must execute the deed. If the trust was created by more than one person the deed must be executed by such of them as are still alive and are of full capacity.[57]

Another exception to the requirement that trustees must consult the beneficiaries arises under the Reverter of Sites Act 1987. Land which is subject to a right of reverter on its ceasing to be used for a particular purpose, vested on trust for sale in the persons in whom it was vested immediately before that use ceased. They held it on trust for those who are entitled to the land on reverter. The land will now be held on trust but express provision is made that the beneficiaries do not have to be consulted before a sale.

The explanation for the exception was given by the Lord Chancellor at Committee Stage in the House of Lords.[58] He said:

'The great advantage of the present provisions of Section 1 of the Reverter of Sites Act 1987 is that they make the position of the trustees very clear and simple in cases where there are often no beneficiaries, only people claiming to be beneficiaries whose entitlement may be difficult to sort out. Irrespective of the identity of the beneficiaries, the trustees can sell the land and, out of the proceeds of sale, deduct all their costs and expenses and meet the capital gains tax liability which they have as trustees. They can sort out the difficult question of entitlement later, if necessary going to court for directions with the proceeds of sale available to cover their costs of doing so in good faith. Under the Reverter of Sites Act, as amended by the Bill at present, however, the question of sale is neutral and there is a duty to consult.

The difficulty which has been identified is that the trustees are put at risk if they sell against the wishes of a claimant who asks for the land to

---

56. Trusts of Land and Appointment of Trustees Act 1996, s 11(4).
57. Ibid, s 11(3).
58. Hansard Vol 570 No 1661 cols 1556 and 1557.

be conveyed to him *in specie* but whose entitlement is in doubt. If that claimant's entitlement is subsequently established in court proceedings, he may sue for loss as a result of the land being sold rather than conveyed to him *in specie*. Trustees will also be faced with the difficulty that if claimants do not wish them to sell and there are difficult issues which need the directions of the court, they may have to incur the costs out of their own resources before they have any proceeds of sale out of which they can be paid.

In view of the fact that the trustees in reverter of sites cases have the trust thrust upon them and will often be such persons as the incumbent and churchwardens (particularly in the case of school sites), there appears to be a strong case for treating this as a special case, rather analogous to the position of personal representatives of a person who dies intestate. Amendments Nos. 31, 32 and 37 accordingly change the existing amendments which the Bill makes to the Reverter of Sites Act so as to ensure that the trust imposed permits the trustees to sell the land and hold the proceeds for the putative beneficiaries without being required to consult them or allow them to occupy the land, and with provision for meeting necessary costs, expenses and taxes.'

5.8   POWER TO DELEGATE

5.8.1   The Trustee Act 1925

The general principle of trust law is that trustees' powers cannot be delegated. The trustee is selected because of his particular qualities. *Delegatus non potest delegare.*

However, trustees have always been entitled to employ agents to act for them for specific transactions. For instance, a trustee can employ a solicitor to do conveyancing work or a stockbroker to buy and sell stocks and shares.

The power of trustees to delegate was extended by s 23 of the Trustee Act 1925. This section provides:

'Trustees or personal representatives may, instead of acting personally, employ and pay an agent, whether a solicitor, banker, stockbroker, or other person, to transact any business or do any act required to be transacted or done in the execution of the trust, or the administration of the testator's or intestate's estate, including the receipt and payment of money, and shall be entitled to be allowed and paid all charges and expenses so incurred, and shall not be responsible for the default of any such agent if employed in good faith.'

However, the section does not confer any power for trustees to delegate their duties generally and it can expressly be excluded by the trust instrument.

A wider statutory power is granted under s 25 of the Trustee Act 1925 as amended by s 9 of the Powers of Attorney Act 1971. The power applies to all trustees, including tenants for life, statutory and personal representatives and to all trusts whenever created. The trustee may by power of attorney delegate for a period not exceeding 12 months all his powers and duties whether vested in him alone or jointly with any other persons. The trustee may not delegate to a sole co-trustee unless that co-trustee is a trust corporation.

Even after delegation the trustee remains liable for the acts and defaults of the person to whom the delegation has been made as if they were his own.

Sections 23 and 25 of the Trustee Act 1925 remain in force, notwithstanding the new power of delegation given to trustees under the Trusts of Land and Appointments of Trustees Act 1996.

5.8.2 The Trusts of Land and Appointment of Trustees Act 1996

Under the Law of Property Act 1925,[59] trustees for sale of land could until sale revocably delegate their powers of leasing, accepting surrenders of leases and management to any person of full age who was for the time being beneficially entitled in possession to the net rents and profits during his life or for any lesser period. The power of sale could not be delegated. The trustees were not liable for the acts or defaults of the person to whom such powers were delegated. The court was given powers to compel such delegation.

The powers under the 1996 Act are wider than under s 29 of the Law of Property Act 1925. That provision is now repealed.

Trustees of land have power to delegate to any beneficiary or beneficiaries of full age who is beneficially entitled to an interest in possession in land subject to the trust, any of their functions as trustees which relate to the land.[60] This includes the power of sale.

A beneficiary who is beneficially entitled is defined as a beneficiary who has an interest in the property subject to the trust and does not include a trustee or personal representative. Nor does it include a beneficiary who is only an annuitant.[61]

The requirement that the beneficiaries be beneficially entitled to an interest in possession prevents any delegation to beneficiaries under a pension trust.

---

59. Law of Property Act 1925, s 29.
60. Trusts of Land and Appointment of Trustees Act 1996, s 9. (For meaning of interest in possession, see *Pearson v IRC* [1981] AC 753, 772 per Viscount Dilhorne 'a present right of present enjoyment'.)
61. Ibid, s 22(2), (3).

The main advantage of the strict settlement is that control is given to the tenant for life, rather than to the trustees. The Law Commission considered that if the power of sale could be delegated, a beneficiary under a trust of land would be given much the same powers as a tenant for life under a strict settlement. However, the effect will not be exactly the same as the delegation will be on a personal revocable basis with the trustees retaining the legal estate. The beneficiary will be acting under a power of attorney.

The power of attorney must be made jointly by all the trustees.[62] Unless it is expressed to be irrevocable and given by way of security, the power of attorney may be revoked by any one or more of the trustees. The power will be automatically revoked by the appointment as a trustee of a person who did not grant the power of attorney. The power will not be revoked if a trustee dies or otherwise ceases to be a trustee. There is no reason in such a situation for the continuing trustees to wish the delegated power to cease at that time.

The need for these provisions was explained by Lord Mishcon at Committee Stage[63] as follows:

'I turn to [subsection (3)]. The principle of the subsection is that all the trustees must at all times be happy with the delegation. A power of attorney must be given by all of them and any one of them can at any time revoke the power under [subsection (3)]. If a new trustee is appointed to the trust, title to the land will become vested in him jointly with the continuing trustees. Any transaction with third parties will therefore show his name as a party along with his co-trustees. In order for a purchaser to be satisfied that the beneficiary purporting to act on the trustees' behalf is empowered to do so, it will be necessary to show that he was appointed by all the current trustees. That will require either an additional provision in the Bill, as I see it, deeming the existing power of attorney to be adopted by a new trustee automatically by virtue of the appointment; or else that the new and continuing trustees grant a renewed power of attorney at or after the time when the appointment of the new trustee takes effect.

Bearing in mind the principle underlying [subsection (3)] to which I referred, I respectfully suggest that it is the latter alternative that would be more appropriate, in order that the matter is not overlooked by the new trustee. Could we have clarification that a power of attorney under Clause 9 automatically loses its effect on the appointment of any new or additional trustee? For my part, I would be quite content that the power of attorney will retain its validity if a trustee simply dies or retires from

---

62. Ibid, s 9(3).
63. Hansard Vol 570 No 1661 col 1538. In the Bill, it was sub-clause 2.

the trust, because in those circumstances there is no reason to suppose that the continuing trustees will necessarily wish the power to terminate at that time, which seems to be implicit in the amended clause.'

Although any trustee may revoke the power of attorney, the provisions under the 1996 Act do not override s 4 of the Powers of Attorney Act 1971. The 1971 Act covers powers of attorney which are expressed to be irrevocable and given by way of security for a proprietary interest of the attorney or for the performance of an obligation owed to him. An example given by the Lord Chancellor[64] where such a power might be used is where there is an employee relocation scheme which operates by a trust mechanism. The power can only be revoked by the consent of the attorney. Powers expressed to be irrevocable and given by way of security are expressly excluded from the revocation provisions of the Trust of Land and Appointment of Trustees Act 1996.

As it is an essential requirement that the beneficiary to whom the powers are delegated is the person beneficially entitled to an interest in possession in the land subject to the trust, should he cease to be so interested, then the power is automatically revoked.[65]

If the functions are delegated to a beneficiary to be exercised by him jointly with other beneficiaries, but not separately, the power is revoked if each of the other beneficiaries cease to be entitled in possession. However, if the other beneficiaries, or some of them, continue to be entitled, they will be able to continue to exercise the delegated functions as long as they retain their qualifying interest. On the other hand, if the functions are delegated to a beneficiary and other beneficiaries to be exercised by them separately or either separately or jointly, the power is revoked only in so far as it related to him.

The delegation may be for a specified period or indefinitely. It cannot, however, be an enduring power of attorney within the meaning of the Enduring Powers of Attorney Act 1985.[66] The essence of the delegation under the 1996 Act is that it is revocable.

The beneficiaries to whom the functions have been delegated are, in relation to the exercise of those functions, in the same position as trustees. In other words, they are subject to the same duties and liabilities. However, such beneficiaries are not considered to be trustees for any other purpose. In particular, they cannot sub-delegate their powers, nor can they give a receipt for the payment of capital money.[67]

Under s 25 of the Trustee Act 1925, which allows for temporary delegation in

---

64. Hansard Vol 572 No 1666 col 95.
65. Trusts of Land and Appointment of Trustees Act 1996, s 9(4).
66. Ibid, s 9(6).
67. Ibid, s 9(7). See Hansard Vol 570 No 1661 cols 1536 and 1537.

a trustee's absence abroad, the trustees in spite of the delegation remain liable. As first drafted, a similar liability was imposed on trustees under the 1996 Act. The three main criticisms of this approach were explained by the Lord Chancellor. He said at Committee Stage:[68]

> 'The first is that the stringent liability, while reasonable in the exceptional circumstances of Section 25 of the Trustee Act 1925, would discourage the use of the power to delegate indefinitely conferred by Clause 9, making the clause a white elephant. The second is that the Law Commission's report envisaged the possibility of a settlor who wishes to get as close as possible to the philosophy of the Settled Land Act actually obliging the trustees to delegate to the income beneficiary, and that this would make it much less likely that anyone would accept a trusteeship in such circumstances (where he could be made liable for the conduct of someone he might have no right to control). The third is that trustees might be forced by a court order to delegate to a beneficiary in the event of dispute, and to hold the trustees liable for a subsequent default by the beneficiary–delegate in those circumstances would be inequitable.
>
> These points have been cogently argued by a variety of commentators both academic and professional, and subsection (7) of the new version of Clause 9 seeks to meet them. The new subsection limits the liabilities of trustees who delegate to circumstances where it was not reasonable for them to delegate to the beneficiary or beneficiaries in question, requiring them to consider whether they should in fact delegate, but freeing them from liability if they are obliged by settlor or court to do so. This narrowing of the liability of trustees is balanced, in the interests of other beneficiaries, by provision in the new subsection (6) for the beneficiary–delegate to be in the position of a trustee, with the concomitant duties and liabilities, in relation to the functions delegated.'

Section 9 was subsequently further amended so that the reference to subsection (7) should now be to subsection (8).

The new provisions as to delegation and the repeal of s 29 of the Law of Property Act 1925 which is consequential on it, do not affect the operation after the commencement of the Act of any delegation which took place before its commencement.[69] This means that any delegation which was effective pursuant to s 29 of the Law of Property Act 1925 will continue to remain effective. Similarly, any acts done by a person to whom powers have been delegated before the commencement pursuant to s 29 will not be affected.

---

68. Hansard Vol 570 No 1661 col 1536.
69. Trusts of Land and Appointment of Trustees Act 1996, s 9(9).

5.9 PERSONAL REPRESENTATIVES

Trusts of land under the 1996 Act, which arise on death, are treated in a similar way to inter vivos trusts. Personal representatives who hold land are not automatically treated as trustees. Both the legal and beneficial interest in the property of the deceased is vested in the personal representatives. The personal representatives are in a fiduciary position and the beneficiaries have a right, if necessary to go to court, to ensure that the assets are duly administered. However, before the completion of the administration the beneficiaries do not have direct equitable interests in the property which is to be distributed.

Personal representatives are therefore given expressly the powers of trustees.[70] This would enable them, for instance, even before the administration of the estate is completed, to use funds to buy a house to accommodate a beneficiary. They will also continue to have the additional functions which are given to personal representatives for the purpose of administration.

The provisions relating to consents, consultation and application to the court for orders under the 1996 Act are inappropriate for personal representatives and are therefore excluded.[71]

Obviously, some modifications of the provisions relating to trustees will be necessary. Two examples are given:

'(a) the substitution of references to persons interested in the due administration of the estate for reference to beneficiaries, and

(b) the substitution of references to the will for references to the disposition creating the trust.'[72]

There are transitional provisions preventing the abolition of the doctrine of conversion applying to personal representatives of a person who dies before the commencement of the Act. If they were treating land under a trust for sale as personalty they will continue to do so.[73]

5.10 POINTS FOR PRACTITIONERS

5.10.1 Consultation – opting out

The provisions for consultation of beneficiaries could prove onerous. In some trusts it may be advisable to provide that beneficiaries need not be consulted. (See Precedent 12.4 in Appendix III.)

---

70. Ibid, s 18(1).
71. Ibid.
72. Ibid, s 18(2).
73. Ibid, s 18(3).

5.10.2 Consultation – opting in

The consultation provisions do not apply to trusts existing at the commencement of the Act. It is possible, however, for settlors to opt in to the provisions for existing trusts. (See Precedent 5 in Appendix III.)

5.10.3 Power of attorney

In order to delegate the powers vested in the trustees, a power of attorney is necessary. (See Precedent 3 in Appendix III.)

5.10.4 Express duty to sell

To avoid applications to court, it may be sensible to incorporate a duty to sell in the trust document. The duty will take precedence over the power to postpone as unanimity is not needed as it is for the exercise of a power. (See Precedent 12.1 in Appendix III.)

5.10.5 Duty to delegate

If the settlor wants the tenant for life of a trust of land to have control of the property he will have to impose in the trust instrument a duty on the trustees to delegate. (See Precedent 12.7 in Appendix III.)

Chapter 6

POWERS OF THE COURT

6.1 LIMITATIONS OF SECTION 30 OF THE LAW OF PROPERTY ACT 1925

Section 30 of the Law of Property Act 1925 provides:

> 'If the trustees for sale refuse to sell or to exercise any of the powers conferred by either of the last two sections, or any requisite consent cannot be obtained, any person interested may apply to the court for a vesting or other order for giving effect to the proposed transaction or for an order directing the trustees for sale to give effect thereto, and the court may make such order as it thinks fit.'

This section has given rise to uncertainties. In the Law Commission Working Paper[1] the following comments were made:

> '[3.19] *Powers conferred by s. 30 of the Law of Property Act 1925.* Problems have arisen with s. 30 of the law of Property Act 1925 as to who can apply under the section, the extent of the powers of the court and the factors to be taken into account in exercising the court's discretion. On the face of it, the section only enables an application to be made if the trustee is refusing to sell. However the courts have found ways of protecting beneficiaries who wish to prevent a sale. It also appears that a trustee who has no beneficial interest in the land may be unable to apply, so that the section does not provide a remedy where the trustees cannot agree to a sale.
>
> [3.20] While the court is given power to make such order as it thinks fit, it is not certain whether this extends to ordering one co-owner who has sole occupation to pay an occupation rent to the other who is not in occupation. It is probably desirable that they should have power to do so, as this provides a possible solution to the problem that where a sale is refused because of the wishes of one co-owner, the other is deprived of a valuable financial asset.
>
> [3.21] A considerable amount of case law exists as to how the discretion should be exercised. Generally the court will look at the purpose for which the trust was created, and see whether the purpose still exists. Particular difficulties have arisen as to the weight to be given to the children's interests, and where one co-owner is bankrupt.'

Sections 14 and 15 of the Trusts of Land and Appointment of Trustees Act 1996 re-enact the effect of s 30 with amendments to ensure that the powers

---

1. Transfer of Land. Trusts of Land (Law Com No 181).

of the court are sufficiently broad and flexible to reflect the nature and purpose of the trust.[2]

6.2   WHO MAY MAKE AN APPLICATION

Any person who is a trustee of land or has an interest in the trust property may make an application.[3] Remaindermen will thus be placed in a much stronger position than they are under a strict settlement. They will be able to apply to the court to challenge any exercise of the trust powers by the trustees or the tenant for life.

A trust of land is defined to include a mixed trust comprising both land and personal property.[4] A person who has an interest in personal property only under the trust may therefore apply.

The section also applies to persons with an interest in a trust of the proceeds of sale of land.[5]

It is not only trustees and beneficiaries who may apply for an order under the Act. A person with an interest covers secured creditors of a beneficiary, such as a person entitled to the benefit of a charging order.

6.3   THE POWERS

Broad powers are given to the court to enable it to make such orders as it thinks fit as to the exercise by the trustees of any of their functions or the nature and extent of the beneficiaries' interests.[6] Under the Trustee Act 1925[7] and the Settled Land Act 1925,[8] the courts already have jurisdiction to add to the powers of trustees.

Although s 30 was interpreted liberally by the courts so as to enable them to settle disputes relating to a trust by giving effect to what they perceived to be the purpose of the trust or the intention of the parties, this was against the underlying duty of the trustees under a trust for sale to sell the property. Moreover, it was generally accepted that the court's power was restricted to ordering or refusing a sale. It was only if it ordered a sale that it could make ancillary orders.

---

2. The case-law on s 30 of the LPA 1925 will be relevant for interpreting the guidelines in s 15. See para **5.3**.
3. Trusts of Land and Appointment of Trustees Act 1996, s 14(1).
4. Ibid, s 1(1)(a).
5. Ibid, s 17(2).
6. Ibid, s 14(2).
7. Trustee Act 1925, s 57.
8. Settled Land Act 1925, s 64.

Once the duty to sell is abolished, it is appropriate that the court should have wider powers. An application can be made to the court to prevent a sale or exercise of a power as well as to enforce a sale or order the exercise of a power. The court may also relieve the trustees of any obligation to obtain the consent of, or to consult, any person in the exercise of their functions.[9]

The powers of the court are exercisable whether the application is made before or after the commencement of the Act. However, any order already made by the court before the commencement will remain unaffected.[10]

6.4 APPOINTMENT OR REMOVAL OF TRUSTEES

The court has no power under s 14 to make an order relating to the appointment or retirement of trustees.[11] The court's jurisdiction in this respect arises under the Trustee Act 1925 and will also be governed by the provisions in Part II of the 1996 Act dealing with the appointment and retirement of trustees.

6.5 DETERMINATION OF APPLICATIONS

6.5.1 General guidelines

In deciding whether to make an order the court has to take into account, among other things, the intentions of the person or persons who created the trust and the purposes for which the trust property is held.[12] In other words, the property need not have been acquired for the purpose. A subsequent purpose may be taken into account.

Another factor which the court must consider is the welfare of any minor who occupies, or might reasonably be expected to occupy, any land subject to the trust as his home. The welfare of the children is thus an independent consideration not linked to the interest of particular beneficial owners. It will not matter in future whether the purpose of the trust was to provide a family home or a matrimonial home.[13]

A further factor for the court to consider is the interests of any secured creditor of a beneficiary.

---

9. Trusts of Land and Appointment of Trustees Act 1996, s 14(2)(a).
10. Ibid, s 14(4).
11. Ibid, s 14(3).
12. Ibid, s 15.
13. Welfare of children is paramount under the Matrimonial and Family Proceedings Act 1984, s 3. Courts have been inconsistent under s 30 of the LPA 1975. Some judges have said that children can only effect outcome in so far as they affect equity of one of the co-owners (see *Rawlings v Rawlings* [1964] P 398; *Burke v Burke* [1974] 1 WLR 1063; *Williams v Williams* [1976] Ch 278).

6.5.2   Applications relating to section 13

In addition to the matters listed in para **6.5.1**, if an application to the court relates to the powers of the trustees to exclude or restrict a beneficiary's right to occupation of the trust property, where two or more beneficiaries are entitled, the court must have regard to the circumstances and wishes of each of the beneficiaries who is, or apart from any previous exercise by the trustees of their powers would be, entitled to occupy the trust land.[14] Taken with the factors in para **6.5.1**, these correspond with the considerations the trustees have to take into account in exercising their powers to exclude or restrict the right to occupy.

6.5.3   Regard to interests of beneficiaries

Where the application does not relate to the trustees' powers to exclude or restrict occupation the court must have regard to the circumstances and wishes of any beneficiaries of full age entitled to an interest in possession in the trust property. If there is disagreement amongst the beneficiaries the court must have regard to the majority according to the value of their combined interests.[15]

This consideration accords with one of the underlying principles of the Act, namely to give greater rights to beneficiaries.

However, the trustees do not have to have regard to the interests of the beneficiaries when the trustees decide to convey the land to the beneficiaries interested in the land where they are all of full age and capacity and between them absolutely entitled to the land. The trustees have the right to terminate the trust and discharge themselves from their obligations where the continuation of the trust is unnecessary, regardless of the wishes of the beneficiaries.

6.6   INSOLVENCY

Where an application is made by a trustee in bankruptcy to the court for an order for sale, the application must be made to the court having jurisdiction in the bankruptcy.

The considerations the court must take into account are those set out in the Insolvency Act 1986 and not those in the Trusts of Land and Appointment of Trustees Act 1996.[16]

On an application the court has power to make such an order as it thinks just and reasonable having regard to:

---

14. Trusts of Land and Appointment of Trustees Act 1996, s 15(2).
15. Ibid, s 15(3).
16. Ibid, s 15(4).

(a) the interests of the bankrupt's creditors;
(b) where the application is made in respect of land which includes a dwellinghouse which is or has been the home of the bankrupt or the bankrupt's spouse or former spouse:
   (i) the conduct of the spouse or former spouse, so far as contributing to the bankruptcy,
   (ii) the needs and financial resources of the spouse or former spouse, and
   (iii) the needs of any children; and
(c) all the circumstances of the case other than the needs of the bankrupt.

Where the application is made after the end of the year beginning with the first vesting of the bankrupt's estate in a trustee, the court will assume, unless there are exceptional circumstances, that the interests of the bankrupt's creditors outweigh all other considerations.[17]

Previously, the guidelines set out in the Insolvency Act 1986 were only applicable where the property was a dwellinghouse held on trust by the bankrupt jointly with a spouse or former spouse. The Act did not cover land in which the bankrupt was beneficially interested but which was held on trust for him by his spouse.

The powers conferred by the new provision are exercisable on an application, whether it is made before or after the commencement of that provision.[18]

---

17. Insolvency Act 1986, s 335A(2), (3) inserted by the Trusts of Land and Appointment of Trustees Act 1996, s 25(1), Sch 3, para 23.
18. Insolvency Act 1986, s 335A(4) inserted by the Trusts of Land and Appointment of Trustees Act 1996, s 25(1), Sch 3, para 23.

Chapter 7

POSITION OF BENEFICIARIES

7.1 MEANING OF BENEFICIARY

A distinction is made in the Act between a beneficiary and a beneficiary who is beneficially entitled.

A beneficiary in relation to a trust means any person who has an interest in the property subject to the trust. This includes trustees and personal representatives.[1]

However, a beneficiary who is beneficially entitled does not include a person whose only interest in the trust is as trustee or personal representative.[2]

An annuitant is beneficially entitled but is not considered to be beneficially entitled to an interest in possession in land subject to the trust.[3]

7.2 PREVIOUS LAW

Before the commencement of the Act, beneficiaries under trusts had limited control of the trust property. In a strict settlement the tenant for life has the legal estate and can make the decisions. However, the position of the remaindermen is weak. They are unable to prevent a sale unless there is lack of good faith. Indeed, the land may have been sold before they are aware of the intention to sell.[4] There is no power under the Settled Land Act 1925 to make the sale of the land, or the exercise of other powers, subject to the consent of the remaindermen or other specified persons.[5]

In a trust for sale the trustees had a duty to consult but this arose only where there was a statutory trust for sale, not an express trust for sale, unless the trust instrument so provided.[6] The trustees only had to give effect to the wishes of the beneficiaries so far as consistent with the general interests of the trust. A purchaser was not affected by the trustees' failure to carry out or comply with the result of any consultation.

The powers of delegation were limited to management and leasing. The powers of sale could not be delegated.[7]

---

1. Trusts of Land and Appointment of Trustees Act 1996, s 22(1).
2. Ibid, s 22(2).
3. Ibid, s 22(3).
4. *England v Public Trustee* (1968) 112 SJ 70.
5. Settled Land Act 1925, s 106.
6. Law of Property Act 1925, s 26(3).
7. Ibid, s 29.

7.3   POSITION STRENGTHENED

Under the Trusts of Land and Appointment of Trustees Act 1996 the beneficiary's position is stronger than that of a beneficiary under a trust for sale. In particular, he has in certain circumstances a right to occupy the land[8] and to give directions on the appointment and retirement of trustees.[9] There is also a provision for the power of sale to be delegated to beneficiaries.[10]

7.4   INTEREST IN LAND RATHER THAN PROCEEDS OF SALE

Where land was held under a trust for sale, the beneficiary's interest was regarded as an interest in the proceeds of sale rather than in the land itself. The historical reason for the doctrine was that before 1925 the law of inheritance on an intestacy differed for personal and real property. It was considered unsatisfactory that a potential beneficiary's position should depend on whether or not the trustees had exercised their duty to sell or not at the date of the death. Therefore, on the basis of the equitable maxim 'equity looks upon that as done which ought to be done', the interest of the beneficiary was treated from the outset as an interest in the proceeds of sale.

The courts, realising that this doctrine is wholly artificial, have not been consistent in their approach.[11]

The 1996 Act abolishes the doctrine of conversion and reverse conversion, whereby interests in money or personal property under a trust are deemed to be an interest in land.[12] The abolition applies to all trusts whenever created, except for trusts created by will where the testator died before the commencement of the Act.

The exception in favour of a testator who died before the commencement of the Act was made in order to ensure that the rules do not operate to produce a result contrary to the intentions of the testator. For example, he may have left all his personal property to X and all his real property to Y. Before the 1996 Act, X would have obtained the land under a trust for sale, but after this Act, Y would do so. If a testator dies after the commencement of the Act, he

---

8. Trusts of Land and Appointment of Trustees Act 1996, s 12.
9. Ibid, s 19.
10. Ibid, s 9.
11. *Re Kempthorne* [1930] 1 Ch 208; *Barclay v Barclay* [1970] 2 QB 677; *Irani Finance v Singh* [1971] Ch 59. Cf *National Westminster Bank v Allen* [1971] 1 QB 718; *Williams & Glyn's Bank v Boland* [1980] 2 All ER 408; *Elias v Mitchell* [1972] Ch 632; *Bull v Bull* [1955] 1 QB 234; *Jones v Jones* [1977] 1 WLR 438; *Cooper v Critchley* [1955] Ch 431; *Cedar Holdings Ltd v Green and Another* [1979] 3 All ER 117.
12. Trusts of Land and Appointment of Trustees Act 1996, s 3.

will have an opportunity to change his will before his death so the potential difficulty can be overcome. The same reasoning applies to inter vivos gifts made before the commencement of the Act.

One consequence of the abolition of the doctrine is that the Revenue will now be able to charge land held under a trust for unpaid inheritance tax. Previously, land held in undivided shares under a trust for sale was exempt along with other personal property.[13]

On the other hand, for the purposes of the Land Charges Act 1972 land continues not to include an undivided share in land. Were the definition to be amended, it would allow registration of a charging order on an interest held as tenant in common. This would be contrary to the intention of the Charging Orders Act 1979 and the policy enshrined in the 1925 legislation of keeping equitable interests off the title.[14] The Land Charges Act 1972 is amended to ensure that a writ or order cannot be registered against any interest under a trust of land.[15]

7.5 RIGHT OF OCCUPATION

7.5.1 The rules

Under the law existing before the commencement of the 1996 Act, it was not clear whether the trustees had power to let beneficiaries occupy the land subject to the trust.[16]

Although under the 1996 Act the trustees are given the powers of absolute owners,[17] without special provision it might not be considered that letting beneficiaries into occupation was a proper exercise of the powers. The Act therefore specifically gives certain beneficiaries the right to occupy such land.[18] This right may be restricted or excluded in certain circumstances.[19]

It is only beneficiaries entitled to an interest in possession in the land who have a right to occupy. This ensures that beneficiaries of pension schemes will not qualify to occupy the land. Those with a purely monetary interest, such an annuitants, are excluded.[20] So are those with a future or contingent interest.

---

13. In the Inheritance Tax Act 1984, s 237(3) the words 'and undivided shares in land held on trust for sale, whether statutory or not' have been repealed.
14. *Perry v Phoenix* [1988] 3 All ER 60 per Browne-Wilkinson VC.
15. Trusts of Land and Appointment of Trustees Act 1996, Sch 3, para 12.
16. Cf *Barclay v Barclay* [1970] 2 QB 677 (express trust for sale) and *Bull v Bull* [1955] 1 QB 234 (statutory trust for sale).
17. Trusts of Land and Appointment of Trustees Act 1996, s 6(1).
18. Ibid, s 12.
19. Ibid, s 13.
20. Ibid, s 22(3).

However, not all such beneficiaries will be entitled to occupation. The purposes of the trust must include making the land available for the occupation of the particular beneficiary, or for the occupation of beneficiaries of a class of which he is a member or for beneficiaries generally. Alternatively, the land must be held by the trustees so as to be available for occupation. It does not have had to be acquired specifically for that purpose. A house might have been acquired for resale but subsequently the trustees might decide not to sell the property but to allow the beneficiary to reside there.

However, although a beneficiary might have a prima facie right to occupation, this can be excluded if the land is unavailable or unsuitable for occupation by him.[21] An example of premises being unsuitable would be where a farm became available but the beneficiary had no farming experience or expertise.

Where two or more beneficiaries have a right to occupy, the trustees have power to regulate the occupation.[22] They may restrict or exclude the right of one or more to occupy the property. However, the trustees cannot exclude the rights of occupation of all the beneficiaries.

In exercising their power to exclude or restrict any beneficiary's right to occupancy, the trustees must not act unreasonably.[23]

Where a beneficiary or beneficiaries have a right to occupy, the trustees may, not just at the beginning of the occupation, but from time to time, impose reasonable conditions.[24] These conditions are not only for protecting the interests of those with competing rights, but also the interests of those beneficiaries who do not have a right to occupy.

When exercising their power to exclude or restrict the right to occupy or to impose conditions, the trustees must take into account, amongst other things:

(a) the intentions of those who created the trust;
(b) the purpose for which the land is held;
(c) the circumstances and wishes of each of the beneficiaries who has a right, or whose right has been excluded or restricted, to occupy the land.[25]

Conditions imposed by the trustees may include an obligation to pay outgoings and rent in respect of the land and to assume any other obligation

---

21. Ibid, s 12(2).
22. Ibid, s 13(1), cf court's power to vary rights of occupation under Matrimonial Homes Act 1983 and Domestic Violence and Matrimonial Proceedings Act 1976.
23. Trusts of Land and Appointment of Trustees Act 1996, s 13(2).
24. Ibid, s 13(3).
25. Ibid, s 13(4).

in respect of the land or to any other activity which is or is proposed to be conducted there.[26]

Where a beneficiary's right to occupy land has been excluded or restricted under s 12, the trustees may impose conditions on any other beneficiary to make payments to him by way of compensation or to benefit him by forgoing any payments or other advantages to which that other beneficiary would otherwise be entitled.[27]

The list of considerations which the Act specifies trustees can impose in respect of the occupation of the land by a beneficiary, or the exclusion and restriction of occupation by other beneficiaries, is not exhaustive.

The difficulty in practice is for the trustees to determine what is the equitable payment.

Under a trust for sale the law was uncertain whether one co-owner who had sole occupation could be ordered by the court to pay an occupation rent to the others who were not in occupation.

The Law Commission made the following comment on occupation rents in its Working Paper:[28]

'If each beneficiary has a right to occupy, should the courts have the power to order, for example, one co-owner to pay money to the other in respect of that occupation? The present law is discussed at some length at first instance in *Dennis v. McDonald* [[1982] Fam. 63 at pp. 70–71], where Purchas J. accepted that "the true position under the old authorities was that the Court of Chancery and Chancery Division would always be ready to inquire into the position as between co-owners being tenants in common either at law or in equity to see whether a tenant in common in occupation of the premises was doing so to the exclusion of one or more of the other tenants in common for whatever purpose or by whatever means. If this was found to be the case, then if in order to do equity between the parties an occupation rent should be paid, this would be declared and the appropriate inquiry ordered. Only in cases where the tenants in common not in occupation were in a position to enjoy their right to occupy but chose not to do so voluntarily, and were not excluded by any relevant factor, would the tenant in common in occupation be entitled to do so free of liability to pay an occupation rent". However, it appears that such a power to require payment of a rent only exists if the situation is one where the court would have power to order a sale. The question that arises is whether

26. Ibid, s 13(5).
27. Ibid, s 13(6).
28. Law Com No 181 footnote 39.

this power should be placed on a statutory footing, or whether it is best to leave the court with the widest powers possible under a re-drafted s. 30. The advantage of legislating is, as always, that it would bring greater certainty, and so make settlements out of court more likely. The disadvantage in this particular case is that to bring greater certainty, one would have to define, with some precision, the situations in which an occupation rent could be paid, and to do so would restrict what is at present a broad jurisdiction. In addition, one might have to lay down principles on which the rent is to be calculated, a matter on which there is relatively little law. Should it be related to the market rent, or to the fair rent as if a tenancy of the dwelling were regulated under the Rent Act 1977 or to the "reasonable rent" as if it were a restricted contract? An alternative measure might be the income lost to the non-occupier through not being able to invest the money he would have received had the property been sold. The circumstances in which the rent might be ordered to be paid seem to be so varied that any attempt at precise definition is likely to lead to unjust results. Accordingly, we suggest that, at most, there should be a provision along the lines that the occupation rent should, so far as equitable and practicable, compensate a beneficiary for his loss of occupation rights.'

A person who is already in occupation whether because he is in occupation under the right to occupy provisions, or for some other reason, is protected. The trustees may not in exercising their powers to exclude or restrict occupation prevent a person either directly or indirectly from continuing in occupation unless that person consents or the court gives approval.[29]

The court in deciding whether to give approval has to take into account the same matters as the trustees do in exercising their powers to exclude or restrict the beneficiaries' occupation of the land (the intentions of the person who created the trust, the purpose for which the land is held and the circumstances and wishes of the beneficiaries who are, or would be, but for restriction or exclusion, entitled to occupy the land).[30]

Beneficiaries or putative beneficiaries under a trust for sale under the Reverter of Sites Act 1987 do not have a right to occupy the trust land.[31]

7.5.2   The effect of overreaching

Although the beneficiary has in certain circumstances a right of occupation against the trustees, this right will not be binding on a purchaser who pays capital money to at least two trustees or a trust corporation. In such

---

29. Trusts of Land and Appointment of Trustees Act 1996, s 13(7).
30. Ibid, s 13(8).
31. Ibid, Sch 3, para 6(2), (6).

circumstances the interest of the beneficiaries will be transferred from the land to the money.

The recommendation of the Law Commission[32] that the interests of adult beneficiaries of full capacity who have a right to occupy trust land, and are in actual occupation of it, should only be overreached if they consent, has not been implemented. However, a person creating a trust can achieve a similar result by stipulating that the trust property shall not be sold without the consent of specified persons.

7.6 TRUSTEES' OBLIGATIONS TO BENEFICIARIES

7.6.1 General law

Trustees must act in accordance with the trust instrument. In addition, trustees are under an obligation to act in the best interests of the beneficiaries. There is a general duty to maintain equality between the beneficiaries and to comply with the equitable rules relating to trusts.[33]

7.6.2 Duty to have regard to the rights of the beneficiaries

In exercising their functions, trustees must have regard to the rights of the beneficiaries.[34] This will be particularly important in relation to the trustees' powers to purchase and sell land.

7.6.3 Duty to obtain consents

A trust instrument may require the consent of specified persons to the exercise of their functions. The specified persons may be beneficiaries. Trustees must comply with the requirement.[35] If they do not, they will be liable for breach of trust.

If the person whose consent is necessary is a minor, the trustees must obtain the consent of a parent who has parental responsibility for him within the meaning of the Children Act 1989 or the child's guardian.[36]

The trustees must also obtain the consent of the beneficiaries before exercising their power to partition the land.[37]

---

32. Transfer of land – Overreaching: Beneficiaries in Occupation (Law Com No 188).
33. See eg *Snell's Equity* 29th edn Ch 6 for the general duties and discretions of trustees.
34. Trusts of Land and Appointment of Trustees Act 1996, s 6(5).
35. Ibid, s 8(2).
36. Ibid, s 10(3)(b). For an explanation on the need to refer to the Children Act 1989 see explanation in annotations to s 10 in Appendix I.
37. Trusts of Land and Appointment of Trustees Act 1996, s 7(3).

7.6.4   Duty to consult

The trustees, in exercise of their functions relating to the trust land, are obliged so far as practicable, to consult the beneficiaries of full age beneficially entitled in possession to an interest in the land, and so far as consistent with the general interest of the trust, to give effect to the wishes of the beneficiaries or a majority of them.[38]

The duty is implied in trusts of land, created after the commencement of the Act, unless the disposition creating the trust provides to the contrary.[39] This reverses the present position under the Law of Property Act 1925.[40] In that Act, where there is an express trust for sale, the need for consultation arises only if the trust instrument so provides. However, there is a statutory requirement to consult where an implied trust for sale is created by statute.

There is no duty to consult where the trustees are exercising their right to convey the land to the beneficiaries on the termination of the trust.[41] This is because it is the policy of the Act to enable the trustees to be discharged where the trust no longer serves any useful purpose. The wishes of the beneficiaries are irrelevant.

The duty to consult does not apply to trusts created or arising under a will made before the commencement of the Act.[42] A testator cannot be expected to rewrite his will to accord with subsequent legislation.

Although the duty to consult does not apply to a trust created inter vivos before the commencement of the Act, or to a trust created subsequently by reference to a pre-Act trust, there are provisions for opting-in.[43] The person who created the trust, provided he is of full capacity, may execute a deed stating that the duty should apply. Where more than one person created the trust, those persons who are alive and of full capacity must all execute the deed. Once executed the deed is irrevocable.[44]

7.6.5   Duty to bring restrictions to attention of purchaser

Trustees have a duty to take reasonable steps to ensure that any restriction on their powers is brought to the attention of prospective purchasers.[45] If the land is registered the trustees should apply for a restriction to be entered on the register of title. Trustees who fail to take reasonable steps will be in breach of trust although purchasers are not affected by an express limitation of the trustees' powers unless they have notice of the limitation.

---

38. Ibid, s 11.
39. Ibid, s 11(2)(a).
40. Law of Property Act 1925, s 26(3).
41. Trusts of Land and Appointment of Trustees Act 1996, s 11(2)(c).
42. Ibid, s 11(2)(b).
43. Ibid, s 11(3).
44. See para **5.7.5**.
45. Trusts of Land and Appointment of Trustees Act 1996, s 16(3).

7.6.6   Delegation of functions to beneficiaries

The purpose of the delegation provision is to enable the functional equivalent of a strict settlement to be achieved by means of a trust of land. In a strict settlement the control, including the power of sale, is given to the tenant for life. In a trust of land, control is given to the trustees unless advantage is taken of the power to delegate. The settlor could stipulate in the trust deed that the power of sale should be delegated.

Trustees of land, including a sole trustee, may delegate any of their functions relating to the land to any person or persons of full age beneficially entitled to an interest in possession in the land.[46] Under the equivalent provision relating to trusts for sale it was not possible to delegate the power of sale.[47]

Trustees are not able to delegate these powers to beneficiaries with a purely monetary interest. An annuitant, although a beneficiary, is not regarded as entitled to an interest in possession in the trust land.[48]

The beneficiary's position is not exactly the same as that of a tenant for life under a strict settlement, since the delegation will be on a personal revocable basis with the trustees retaining the legal estate. The beneficiary will be dealing with the estate as attorney only.[49]

Although beneficiaries to whom the trustees' functions have been delegated are, in relation to those functions, in the same position as trustees, they are not regarded as trustees for any other purpose. In particular, they cannot sub-delegate, nor can they give a receipt for capital money.[50]

7.7   DIRECTIONS TO TRUSTEES

Where there is no person nominated for the purposes of appointing new trustees by the trust instrument and all the beneficiaries are of full age and capacity and together absolutely entitled to the trust property, they may direct the appointment and retirement of trustees[51] unless there is a contrary intention in the trust instrument.[52]

The power exists in all trusts of personal and real property even if they were created before the commencement of the Act unless a deed is executed stating that the rules shall not apply.[53]

---

46. Ibid, s 9.
47. Law of Property Act 1925, s 29.
48. Trusts of Land and Appointment of Trustees Act 1996, ss 9(1) and 22(3).
49. For an explanation of the power of delegation see para **5.8.2**.
50. Trusts of Land and Appointment of Trustees Act 1996, s 9(7).
51. Ibid, s 19(1).
52. Ibid, s 21(5).
53. Ibid, s 21(6).

7.8 ENFORCED TERMINATION OF THE TRUST

Although before the commencement of the Act it was considered that beneficiaries could not control the appointment or retirement of the trustees, beneficiaries of full age and capacity could, if together they were absolutely entitled, bring the trust to an end. This right continues.[54]

The Act, however, goes further and provides that where beneficiaries are of full age and capacity and are absolutely entitled to the land, the trustees may force the beneficiaries to accept a conveyance of the land, with the help of the court if necessary.[55] This enables the trustees to bring a trust to an end where its continuation is unnecessary. Because this power is exercisable, whether or not the beneficiaries so require, it is not subject to the duty to consult.

The beneficiaries are under a duty to do whatever is necessary to secure that the property vests in them. This will include, for example, applying to the Land Registry to have the transfer registered if the title to the land is already registered. It would not be an occasion for compulsory registration where the title to the land is not registered.

If the beneficiaries fail to do what is required to vest title in themselves, the court may make an order ordering them to do so.

7.9 POWER TO APPLY TO THE COURT

A beneficiary, amongst other persons, may make an application to the court in the event of dispute, or uncertainty concerning a trust of land.[56] A beneficiary of a mixed trust of land and personal property may apply even if his interest is only in personal property and not in land.[57] The power also applies where it is a trust of the proceeds of sale of land.[58]

The beneficiary can seek an order relating to the exercise by the trustees of their functions, as well as the nature and extent of the beneficiary's interest. However, the court cannot make an order concerning the appointment or removal of trustees.[59]

In making any order the court must pay regard to a number of factors, including the intentions of the person who created the trust, the purposes for which the property subject to the trust is held, the welfare of any minor who occupies or might reasonably be expected to occupy any land subject to

54. *Saunders v Vautier* (1841) 4 Beav 115.
55. Trusts of Land and Appointment of Trustees Act 1996, s 6(2).
56. Ibid, s 14.
57. Trusts of Land and Appointment of Trustees Act 1996, s 1.
58. Ibid, s 17(2).
59. Ibid, s 14(3).

the trust as his home, and the interests of any secured creditor of the beneficiary.[60]

In addition, where the application relates to the trustees' powers to restrict or exclude the beneficiaries' right of occupation, the court must have regard to the circumstances and wishes of each of the beneficiaries entitled to occupy the land and of those beneficiaries who would have been entitled to occupy, had the trustees not previously exercised their powers to exclude or restrict them.[61]

Where the application relates to other matters, the court must have regard to, amongst other things, the circumstances and wishes of any beneficiaries of full age entitled to an interest in possession in the property subject to the trust.[62] Where the beneficiaries are in dispute, the court must pay attention to the circumstances and wishes of the majority according to their combined interests. The wishes and circumstances of the beneficiaries are not taken into account where the matters in dispute relate to the power of the trustees to vest the property in the beneficiaries on the termination of the trust. The trustees have no obligation to consult the beneficiaries before exercising that power as the trustees can vest the property in the beneficiaries, even against their wishes. This is to enable the trustees to discharge themselves from the trust where it no longer serves any useful purpose.

7.10   POINTS FOR PRACTITIONERS

7.10.1   Exclusion of rights of beneficiaries in new trusts

The person who creates the trust may want to exclude some of the rights of the beneficiaries. Clauses are given in Precedent 12 in Appendix III for excluding or restricting statutory powers and requiring consents under s 8(1), (2), excluding or restricting obligations to consult beneficiaries under s 11(2)(a), excluding or restricting beneficiaries' right to occupy land under s 12 and excluding or restricting trustees' appointment provisions under s 21(5).

7.10.2   Opting-out of appointment provisions for existing trusts

Section 21(6) enables a person or persons who created the trust to opt out of the provisions for the appointment and retirement of a trustee. (See Precedent 11 in Appendix III.)

---

60. Ibid, s 15(1).
61. Ibid, s 15(2).
62. Ibid, s 15(3).

Chapter 8

PROTECTION OF THE PURCHASER

8.1   INTRODUCTION

'Purchaser' in the Trusts of Land and Appointment of Trustees Act 1996 has the same meaning as in Part I of the Law of Property Act 1925. In that Act,[1] purchaser is defined as:

> 'Purchaser ... means a person who acquires an interest or charge on property for money or money's worth.'

A purchaser is protected in several ways. If he pays the purchase money to two trustees or a trust corporation he will take free of the equitable interests.[2] He is not concerned to see that the trustees have followed all the requirements of the Act relating to consents and consultation.[3] In addition, where he lacks actual knowledge, he is not bound by any restrictions or limitations imposed by the trust instrument or by any enactment or rule of law restricting the trustees' powers.[4] There are also provisions which will protect a purchaser where the trustees' powers have been delegated to a beneficiary.[5] Finally, he can assume that the trust has terminated if there is a deed of discharge.[6]

These provisions uphold the established principle that a purchaser should not be required to examine the trust instrument to determine the validity of the conveyance.

8.2   OVERREACHING

8.2.1   Trusts for sale and strict settlements

The principal protection for a purchaser of land lies in the doctrine of overreaching. Provided the purchaser pays the capital money to at least two trustees or a trust corporation, he will take free of the equitable interests under the trust. The beneficiaries' interests are transferred from the land to the proceeds of sale.[7]

Where the purchaser fails to pay the capital money to two trustees, the position differs according to whether the legal estate is held by the trustees

---

1. Law of Property Act 1925, s 205(xxi).
2. Ibid, ss 2, 27. Trusts of Land and Appointment of Trustees Act 1996, Sch 3, para 4.
3. Ibid, s 16(1).
4. Ibid, s 16(2), (3).
5. Ibid, s 9(2).
6. Ibid, s 16(5).
7. Law of Property Act 1925, ss 2, 27.

upon trust for sale or by the tenant for life or statutory owners under a strict settlement.

In a trust for sale, where the title to the land is unregistered a purchaser takes free of the equitable interests if he is a bona fide purchaser of the legal estate, without notice of them. If he did have notice he would take subject to them.

On the other hand, in a strict settlement, if a purchaser fails to pay the capital money to two trustees the conveyance is void except in so far as it binds the beneficial interest of the life tenant.[8] To some extent the purchaser may be protected by s 110 of the Settled Land Act 1925. However, it is not certain whether s 110, which provides that a purchaser dealing in good faith with a tenant for life shall be taken to have complied with all the requisitions of the Act, requires the purchaser to know that he is dealing with the tenant for life. It is also uncertain whether the protection is available where the disposition is void. In other words, whether s 18 or s 110 prevails.

Where title to land is registered, a purchaser's position depends on whether or not there is an entry on the register.[9] If there is a restriction requiring capital money to be paid to two trustees the purchaser will not obtain a good title unless he complies with that restriction. The interest under the trust, whether it is a strict settlement or trust for sale may also be protected by a caution. If the caution is correctly lodged, then in order for the title to be perfected, a second trustee will have to be appointed.

It is also possible that the purchaser will take subject to the interest of the beneficiary, even if there is no restriction on the register. A beneficiary in occupation under a trust for sale will have an overriding interest which will bind a purchaser whether he knows about it or not.[10] Successive or other interests under a strict settlement cannot amount to overriding interests.[11]

8.2.2   Trusts of land

Overreaching applies to trusts of land in the same way as it did to trusts for sale and strict settlements. Moreover, it applies to a bare trust which comes within the definition of a trust of land.[12] Before the passing of the Act, interests under a bare trust could not be overreached, even if a purchaser paid capital money to at least two trustees.

If a purchaser fails to pay the capital money to two trustees or a trust corporation, the conveyance will not be invalid. A purchaser will take subject

---

8. Settled Land Act 1925, s 18.
9. Land Registration Act 1925, s 20.
10. Ibid, s 70(1)(g).
11. Ibid, s 86(2).
12. Trusts of Land and Appointment of Trustees Act 1996, s 1(2) and Sch 3, para 4.

to the equitable interests unless he can show that he is a bona fide purchaser of the legal estate without notice of the interests.

If the title to the land is registered and there is a restriction requiring capital money to be paid to at least two trustees, a purchaser will not get a good title unless he complies with the restriction. Either the trustees or the beneficiaries can apply to register a restriction.[13]

8.3 PURCHASERS NOT CONCERNED WITH ALL TRUSTEES' OBLIGATIONS

8.3.1 Regard to the rights of the beneficiaries

In exercising their general powers the trustees are under a duty to have regard to the rights of the beneficiaries.[14] However, a purchaser is not concerned to see that this duty has been complied with.[15]

8.3.2 Consultation

In certain circumstances, the trustees are under a duty in the exercise of any functions relating to land subject to the trust to consult the beneficiaries of full age who are beneficially entitled to an interest in possession. Having consulted them, the trustees are under an obligation to give effect to their wishes so far as is consistent with the general interest of the trust. The purchaser is not concerned to see if such consultation has taken place.[16]

8.3.3 Consents

The trustees have a power to partition the trust land where the beneficiaries are of full age and absolutely entitled as tenants in common. They then must convey the partitioned land to each person in accordance with his rights. However, before making the partition, the trustees have to obtain the consent of each of the beneficiaries. A purchaser is not concerned to see if such consent is obtained.[17]

Sometimes a trust instrument will state that the consent of specified persons are needed before the trustees exercise their powers. The consent of any two persons is sufficient for the purposes of a purchaser.[18] The trustees, however, will be liable for breach of trust should all the specified consents not be obtained.

---

13. Ibid, Sch 3, para 5(8).
14. Ibid, s 6(5).
15. Ibid, s 16(1).
16. Ibid, ss 11(1), 16(1).
17. Ibid, ss 7(3), 16(1).
18. Ibid, s 10(1).

Where the consent of a minor is required to the exercise of a function of the trustees of land, his consent is not necessarily in favour of a purchaser but the trustees are under a duty to obtain the consent of his parent or guardian.[19]

8.3.4 Limitations imposed by the trust instrument

The trust instrument may limit the powers of the trustees. It may cut down the general powers of the trustees including their power to purchase or partition land. It may also provide that the powers cannot be exercised without consent.

The trustees are under a duty to take all reasonable steps to bring the limitation to the notice of any purchaser. However, the limitation will not invalidate any conveyance by the trustees to a purchaser who has no actual notice of the limitation.[20]

Where title to land is registered, trustees should apply for a restriction to be entered on the register. Failure to do so might amount to a breach of trust.

Beneficiaries with unco-operative trustees may themselves apply for a restriction or caution to protect their interests.[21] There is no equivalent procedure available to purchasers with an interest in unregistered land. The beneficiaries will have to rely on an action for breach of trust.

8.3.5 Limitations imposed by law

The powers of the trustees may be prohibited by an enactment or order made thereunder or rule of law or equity, or the law may make the powers subject to restrictions, limitations or conditions. However, any conveyance in contravention of the prohibitions, restrictions, limitations or conditions will not be invalidated where the purchaser of the land from the trustees has no actual knowledge of the contravention.[22]

An example of the operation of the rule is where a beneficiary, being of full age and capacity and absolutely entitled, requests the trustees to convey the legal estate to him but the trustees in breach of trust convey the land to a third party. Provided the purchaser had no actual notice the conveyance would be valid, but the beneficiary could sue the trustees for breach of trust.

---

19. Ibid, s 10(3)(a), (b).
20. Ibid, ss 8, 16(3).
21. Ibid, Sch 3, para 5(8).
22. Ibid, s 16(3).

8.4 PROTECTION WHERE TRUSTEES' POWERS DELEGATED

Trustees of land may delegate their functions as trustees to a beneficiary or beneficiaries entitled to an interest in possession of the land.[23] Delegation is by way of power of attorney. A third party dealing in good faith with the beneficiary, with the delegated powers, is entitled to assume, unless he has knowledge to the contrary at the time the transaction was entered into, that the delegate is a person to whom the delegation could be properly made. It is conclusively presumed in favour of a purchaser whose interest depends on the validity of the transaction between the beneficiary–delegate and a third party that the third party dealt in good faith and did not have knowledge that the powers could not have been delegated to that beneficiary if a statutory declaration is made to that effect by the third party. The declaration must be made before or within three months of the completion of the purchase by the purchaser.[24]

If the power of attorney is revoked the purchaser (or other person) will be protected in his dealings with the beneficiary if he has no knowledge of the revocation. Any subsequent purchaser can presume that the first purchaser (or other person) did not know of the revocation if the transaction between the beneficiary and the purchaser was completed within 12 months of the date on which the power came into operation or the first purchaser (or other person) makes a statutory declaration before or within three months of the purchase that he did not at the material time know of the revocation of the power.[25]

8.5 TERMINATION OF THE TRUST

8.5.1 Termination of a strict settlement

On the termination of a strict settlement, that is where an estate owner holds the land free from other equitable interests under the trusts, the trustees are bound to execute a deed declaring that they are discharged from the trusts. A purchaser can rely on this and assume that the land is no longer settled land.[26]

8.5.2 Termination of a trust for sale

There was no similar provision on the termination of a trust for sale. Even where the trust had come to an end, a purchaser would only get a good title if

---

23. Ibid, s 9(1).
24. Ibid, s 9(2).
25. Power of Attorney Act 1971, s 5.
26. Settled Land Act 1925, s 17 (see also s 110(5)).

he paid his money to two trustees or a trust corporation.[27] The alternative was for the purchaser to investigate the equitable title to ensure that the trust has truly terminated. This is of course contrary to the principle of the 1925 legislation which was to keep the equitable interests behind the curtain.

8.5.3   Termination of a trust of land

One of the powers of trustees in a trust of land is to convey the land to the beneficiaries where they are of full age and capacity and absolutely entitled to the land. This power can be exercised even where the beneficiaries have not requested the trustees to do so. After such a conveyance, the trustees are bound to execute a deed declaring that they are discharged from the trust in relation to that land. If they fail to execute the deed the court has the power to order them to do so.

A purchaser is entitled to assume that from the date of the deed the land is not subject to the trust, unless he has actual knowledge that the trustees were mistaken in their belief that the beneficiaries were of full age and capacity and absolutely entitled.[28]

If the title to the land is registered the purchaser will get a good title if the equitable interests under the trust are not protected by a restriction or caution and the beneficiary is not in occupation. A beneficiary in occupation would have an overriding interest which would bind a purchaser whether he knew of it or not.[29]

8.6   CHARITABLE, ECCLESIASTICAL AND PUBLIC TRUSTS

Where ss 37(1), (2) and 39(1), (2) of the Charities Act 1993 do not apply, a purchaser from trustees of charitable, ecclesiastical and public trusts must ensure that the trustees have power to convey the land and that all restrictions, limitations and conditions have been complied with, whether imposed as a matter of law or by the terms of the trust.[30]

A conveyance must state that the land is held on such trusts and where a purchaser has notice that the land is so held he must satisfy himself that the necessary consents have been obtained.

Trustees holding registered land under charitable trusts should enter an appropriate restriction on the register.

---

27. The only exception is where there is a surviving joint tenant who complied with the Law of Property (Joint Tenants) Act 1964.
28. Trusts of Land and Appointment of Trustees Act 1996, s 16(5).
29. Land Registration Act 1925, ss 20, 70(1)(g).
30. Trusts of Land and Appointment of Trustees Act 1996, Sch 1, para 4. For notes on the Charities Act 1993, see annotations to s 2 and Sch 1, para 4.

8.7 POINTS FOR PRACTITIONERS

Most of the new legislation on the protection of purchasers is the same as existed under the old rules relating to trusts for sale.

8.7.1 Deed of discharge

However, the important new provision is the deed of discharge on which the purchaser can rely when a trust of land is terminated. (See Precedent 6 in Appendix III.)

8.7.2 Statutory declaration

A purchaser whose title depends on a previous transaction between a beneficiary to whom the trustees' powers have been delegated and a third party should ensure that he obtains a statutory declaration from the third party to the effect that he acted in good faith and had no knowledge that the beneficiary was not of full age and entitled to an interest in possession. (See Precedent 4 in Appendix III.)

Appendix 1

Trusts of Land and Appointment of Trustees Act 1996
(1996 c 47)

ARRANGEMENT OF SECTIONS

TRUSTS OF LAND

Introductory

Section		Page
1	Meaning of 'trust of land'	82

Settlements and trusts for sale as trusts of land

2	Trusts in place of settlements	83
3	Abolition of doctrine of conversion	84
4	Express trusts for sale as trusts of land	84
5	Implied trusts for sale as trusts of land	85

Functions of trustees of land

6	General powers of trustees	85
7	Partition by trustees	87
8	Exclusion and restriction of powers	87
9	Delegation by trustees	88

Consents and consultation

| 10 | Consents | 90 |
| 11 | Consultation with beneficiaries | 91 |

Right of beneficiaries to occupy trust land

| 12 | The right to occupy | 92 |
| 13 | Exclusion and restriction of right to occupy | 92 |

Powers of court

| 14 | Applications for order | 94 |
| 15 | Matters relevant in determining applications | 94 |

Purchaser protection

| 16 | Protection of purchasers | 95 |

Supplementary

17   Application of provisions to trusts of proceeds of sale   96
18   Application of Part to personal representatives   97

PART II
APPOINTMENT AND RETIREMENT OF TRUSTEES

19   Appointment and retirement of trustee at instance of beneficiaries   98
20   Appointment of substitute for incapable trustee   99
21   Supplementary   100

PART III
SUPPLEMENTARY

22   Meaning of 'beneficiary'   101
23   Other interpretation provisions   101
24   Application to Crown   102
25   Amendments, repeals etc.   102
26   Power to make consequential provision   103
27   Short title, commencement and extent   103
     SCHEDULES:
     Schedule 1—Provisions consequential on section 2   105
     Schedule 2—Amendments of statutory provisions imposing trust for
                 sale   107
     Schedule 3—Minor and consequential amendments   111
     Schedule 4—Repeals   121

An Act to make new provision about trusts of land including provision phasing out the Settled Land Act 1925, abolishing the doctrine of conversion and otherwise amending the law about trusts for sale of land; to amend the law about the appointment and retirement of trustees of any trust; and for connected purposes.

[24th July 1996]

PART I
TRUSTS OF LAND

Introductory

1 Meaning of 'trust of land'

(1) In this Act—

    (a)   'trust of land' means (subject to subsection (3)) any trust of property which consists of or includes land, and

    (b)   'trustees of land' means trustees of a trust of land.

(2) The reference in subsection (1)(a) to a trust—

    (a)   is to any description of trust (whether express, implied, resulting or constructive), including a trust for sale and a bare trust, and

(b)   includes a trust created, or arising, before the commencement of this Act.

(3) The reference to land in subsection (1)(a) does not include land which (despite section 2) is settled land or which is land to which the Universities and College Estates Act 1925 applies.

Explanatory text—See para **3.1**.

A 'trust of land' means:

(1)   a trust of land alone:
(2)   a mixed trust of land and personalty,

whether (1) or (2) is an express, implied, resulting, constructive trust, a trust for sale or a bare trust and whether arising before or after the commencement of the Act.

Consequential amendments to the Law of Property Act 1925 are made in Sch 3 to ensure that the statutory overreaching machinery applies to all trusts of land including bare trusts.

A bare trust is where property is held by a trustee who has no interest in or duty as to the property other than to convey it when required according to the directions of the beneficial owner.

Excluded from the Act are strict settlements and land which is governed by the Universities and College Estates Act 1925.

Settlements and trusts for sale as trusts of land

2   Trusts in place of settlements

(1) No settlement created after the commencement of this Act is a settlement for the purposes of the Settled Land Act 1925; and no settlement shall be deemed to be made under that Act after that commencement.

(2) Subsection (1) does not apply to a settlement created on the occasion of an alteration in any interest in, or of a person becoming entitled under, a settlement which—

(a)   is in existence at the commencement of this Act, or
(b)   derives from a settlement within paragraph (a) or this paragraph.

(3) But a settlement created as mentioned in subsection (2) is not a settlement for the purposes of the Settled Land Act 1925 if provision to the effect that it is not is made in the instrument, or any of the instruments, by which it is created.

(4) Where at any time after the commencement of this Act there is in the case of any settlement which is a settlement for the purposes of the Settled Land Act 1925 no relevant property which is, or is deemed to be, subject to the settlement, the settlement permanently ceases at that time to be a settlement for the purposes of that Act.

In this subsection 'relevant property' means land and personal chattels to which section 67(1) of the Settled Land Act 1925 (heirlooms) applies.

(5) No land held on charitable, ecclesiastical or public trusts shall be or be deemed to be settled land after the commencement of this Act, even if it was or was deemed to be settled land before that commencement.

(6) Schedule 1 has effect to make provision consequential on this section (including provision to impose a trust in circumstances in which, apart from this section, there

would be a settlement for the purposes of the Settled Land Act 1925 (and there would not otherwise be a trust)).

Explanatory text—See para **3.3**.

Subsection (1)—A deemed settlement arises through the operation of statutory provisions, eg charitable trusts or conveyances to minors. Deemed settlements are specifically mentioned as it is arguable that settlements arising through statute are not created.

Subsections (2) and (3)—Subject to a contrary intention in the trust instrument, where new land is brought into an existing strict settlement, it will continue to be governed by the Settled Land Act 1925. So will resettlements of existing settlements and resettlements of resettlements and the exercise of a power of appointment under a strict settlement.

For a clause which has the effect of excluding the trust from the application of the Settled Land Act 1925, see Precedent 12.2 in Appendix III.

Subsection (4)—After there has ceased to be any land or heirlooms subject to a strict settlement, any land or settled chattels which subsequently become subject to the settlement will be held on trust. This enables the phasing out of strict settlements.

Subsection (5)—Charitable, ecclesiastical and public trusts were deemed to be strict settlements only for the purposes of s 29. They will now become trusts of land.

Subsection (6)—Schedule 1 deals with minors, family charges, charitable, ecclesiastical and public trusts, entailed interests and the position where there is no longer any relevant property subject to a settlement. It provides that where formerly there was a strict settlement after the commencement of the Act there will be a trust of land.

3 Abolition of doctrine of conversion

(1) Where land is held by trustees subject to a trust for sale, the land is not to be regarded as personal property; and where personal property is subject to a trust for sale in order that the trustees may acquire land, the personal property is not to be regarded as land.

(2) Subsection (1) does not apply to a trust created by a will if the testator died before the commencement of this Act.

(3) Subject to that, subsection (1) applies to a trust whether it is created, or arises, before or after that commencement.

Explanatory text—See para **2.2.3**.

The doctrine of conversion and reversed conversion is abolished for all trusts whenever created except where the trust was created by will and the testator died before the commencement of the Act.

4 Express trusts for sale as trusts of land

(1) In the case of every trust for sale of land created by a disposition there is to be implied, despite any provision to the contrary made by the disposition, a power for the trustees to postpone sale of the land; and the trustees are not liable in any way for postponing sale of the land, in the exercise of their discretion, for an indefinite period.

(2) Subsection (1) applies to a trust whether it is created, or arises, before or after the commencement of this Act.

(3) Subsection (1) does not affect any liability incurred by trustees before that commencement.

Explanatory text—See para **3.6**.

Any trust for sale, whether created before or after the commencement of the Act, gives the trustees a power to postpone the sale, notwithstanding any provision to the contrary. There will still be a duty to sell, so one trustee could insist on a sale even against the wishes of the others (*Re Mayo* [1943] Ch 302), cf a power when the trustees must be unanimous.

Cf Law of Property Act, s 25 where there was a power to postpone unless there was a contrary intention.

5 Implied trusts for sale as trusts of land

(1) Schedule 2 has effect in relation to statutory provisions which impose a trust for sale of land in certain circumstances so that in those circumstances there is instead a trust of the land (without a duty to sell).

(2) Section 1 of the Settled Land Act 1925 does not apply to land held on any trust arising by virtue of that Schedule (so that any such land is subject to a trust of land).

Explanatory text—See para **3.7**.

There will no longer be any implied trusts for sale. These are converted into trusts of land without a duty to sell.

Subsection (1)—Where mortgaged property is held by trustees after the redemption is barred, land is purchased by trustees of personal property, there is a disposition to tenants in common, land is held in trust for joint tenants, personal representatives hold an intestate's estate or land is held by trustees under the Reverter of Sites Act 1987, a trust for sale was imposed by statute. Now a trust of land without a duty to sell will be imposed.

Subsection 1 brings into effect Sch 2. Refer to that Schedule for a commentary on the individual amendments effected by it.

Functions of trustees of land

6 General powers of trustees

(1) For the purpose of exercising their functions as trustees, the trustees of land have in relation to the land subject to the trust all the powers of an absolute owner.

(2) Where in the case of any land subject to a trust of land each of the beneficiaries interested in the land is a person of full age and capacity who is absolutely entitled to the land, the powers conferred on the trustees by subsection (1) include the power to convey the land to the beneficiaries even though they have not required the trustees to do so; and where land is conveyed by virtue of this subsection—

  (a)   the beneficiaries shall do whatever is necessary to secure that it vests in them, and
  (b)   if they fail to do so, the court may make an order requiring them to do so.

(3) The trustees of land have power to purchase a legal estate in any land in England or Wales.

(4) The power conferred by subsection (3) may be exercised by trustees to purchase land—

    (a)   by way of investment,

    (b)   for occupation by any beneficiary, or

    (c)   for any other reason.

(5) In exercising the powers conferred by this section trustees shall have regard to the rights of the beneficiaries.

(6) The powers conferred by this section shall not be exercised in contravention of, or of any order made in pursuance of, any other enactment or any rule of law or equity.

(7) The reference in subsection (6) to an order includes an order of any court or of the Charity Commissioners.

(8) Where any enactment other than this section confers on trustees authority to act subject to any restriction, limitation or condition, trustees of land may not exercise the powers conferred by this section to do any act which they are prevented from doing under the other enactment by reason of the restriction, limitation or condition.

Explanatory text—See paras **5.2–5.5**.

This section is derived from ss 23 and 28 of the LPA 1925 which are repealed.

Subsection (2)—This gives statutory force to a provision commonly found in trust documents. Absolute owners have powers to sell or retain the land. The powers are, however, subject to the overriding principle that the trustees must act in a trustee-like manner. This is made clear by the words at the beginning of the section 'For the purpose of exercising their functions as trustees'.

    The statutory restrictions on the trustees' power to insure land and buildings is removed as a consequence of the trustees having the powers of absolute owners. See amendment to s 19 of the Trustee Act 1925 by Sch 3, para 3(4).

Subsection (2)—Where beneficiaries with concurrent interests are absolutely entitled, either as joint tenants or tenants in common, provided they are of full age and capacity, the trustees can compel them to take a conveyance of the trust property. The beneficiaries must do what is necessary to vest the property in them, eg by applying for registration of title.

    No consultation with the beneficiaries is required (s 11(2)(c)).

    For a conveyance of land to beneficiaries absolutely entitled in pursuance of s 6(2), see Precedent 1 in Appendix III.

Subsection (3)—This reproduces existing law (see Law of Property Act 1925, s 28(1); Settled Land Act 1925, s 73(2)). If the person who creates the trust wants to allow the trustees to purchase foreign land he will have to so provide in the trust instrument. The powers are available not only to the trustees of land but also to the trustees of the proceeds of the sale of land (s 17(1)). The power to purchase land is not therefore dependent on land being currently held by the trustees.

Subsection (4)—Broad and flexible powers are given to the trustees to purchase of land for any purposes.

Subsection (5)—This provides protection for the beneficiaries but is of no concern to the purchasers (s 16(1)).

Subsections (6), (7) and (8)—The wide powers given under subsection (1) are subject to any limitations in other enactments or rules of law or equity, eg Trustee Act 1925; Trustee Investment Act 1961.

7 Partition by trustees

(1) The trustees of land may, where beneficiaries of full age are absolutely entitled in undivided shares to land subject to the trust, partition the land, or any part of it, and provide (by way of mortgage or otherwise) for the payment of any equality money.

(2) The trustees shall give effect to any such partition by conveying the partitioned land in severalty (whether or not subject to any legal mortgage created for raising equality money), either absolutely or in trust, in accordance with the rights of those beneficiaries.

(3) Before exercising their powers under subsection (2) the trustees shall obtain the consent of each of those beneficiaries.

(4) Where a share in the land is affected by an incumbrance, the trustees may either give effect to it or provide for its discharge from the property allotted to that share as they think fit.

(5) If a share in the land is absolutely vested in a minor, subsections (1) to (4) apply as if he were of full age, except that the trustees may act on his behalf and retain land or other property representing his share in trust for him.

Explanatory text—See para **5.6**.

This section is derived from the LPA 1925, s 28(3) and (4). It applies where beneficiaries are entitled as tenants in common. If the trustees or any of the beneficiaries refuse to consent to a partition, an application can be made to the court under s 14. A purchaser is not concerned to see that any consent has been obtained (s 16(1)).

For a conveyance upon partition, see Precedent 2 in Appendix III.

8 Exclusion and restriction of powers

(1) Sections 6 and 7 do not apply in the case of a trust of land created by a disposition in so far as provision to the effect that they do not apply is made by the disposition.

(2) If the disposition creating such a trust makes provision requiring any consent to be obtained to the exercise of any power conferred by section 6 or 7, the power may not be exercised without that consent.

(3) Subsection (1) does not apply in the case of charitable, ecclesiastical or public trusts.

(4) Subsections (1) and (2) have effect subject to any enactment which prohibits or restricts the effect of provision of the description mentioned in them.

Explanatory text—See para **5.7.1**.

Subsections (1), (2) and (3)—The trust instrument may restrict the powers of the trustees unless it is a charitable, ecclesiastical or public trust. The powers given in the 1996 Act do not override any other enactments, eg the Trustee Investment Act 1961. If the trust instrument specifies consents they must be obtained.

Failure to obtain consents will amount to a breach of trust. Where more than two consents are required the consent of any two is sufficient in favour of a purchaser (s 10(1)).

If the land is unregistered and there are limitations, a purchaser will not be bound by them unless he has actual notice (s 16(3)). If it is registered then there should be a restriction on the register (Sch 3, para 5(8)(c)).

Not only the trustees but also the beneficiaries can apply for a restriction. This is a similar provision for settled land under s 86 of the Land Registration Act 1925.

Trustees are under an obligation to bring the limitation to the notice of any purchaser (s 16(3)).

For a form of clause excluding or restricting the statutory powers of the trustee, see Precedent 12.3 in Appendix III.

Subsection (3)—This restores the effect of s 106 of the SLA 1925 for these trusts. Charities must operate as efficiently as possible and should not be impeded by restrictions which might result in applications having to be made to the Charity Commissioners.

Subsection (4)—This subsection was included to prevent particular provisions in occupational pension schemes being thwarted. It is drafted in more general terms to ensure that similar provisions in other legislation are not adversely affected. Section 35(4) of the Pensions Act 1995 prevents the powers of occupational pension scheme trustees being fettered by requirements to obtain the consent of the employer.

9 Delegation by trustees

(1) The trustees of land may, by power of attorney, delegate to any beneficiary or beneficiaries of full age and beneficially entitled to an interest in possession in land subject to the trust any of their functions as trustees which relate to the land.

(2) Where trustees purport to delegate to a person by a power of attorney under subsection (1) functions relating to any land and another person in good faith deals with him in relation to the land, he shall be presumed in favour of that other person to have been a person to whom the functions could be delegated unless that other person has knowledge at the time of the transaction that he was not such a person.

And it shall be conclusively presumed in favour of any purchaser whose interest depends on the validity of that transaction that that other person dealt in good faith and did not have such knowledge if that other person makes a statutory declaration to that effect before or within three months after the completion of the purchase.

(3) A power of attorney under subsection (1) shall be given by all the trustees jointly and (unless expressed to be irrevocable and to be given by way of security) may be revoked by any one or more of them; and such a power is revoked by the appointment as a trustee of a person other than those by whom it is given (though not by any of those persons dying or otherwise ceasing to be a trustee).

(4) Where a beneficiary to whom functions are delegated by a power of attorney under subsection (1) ceases to be a person beneficially entitled to an interest in possession in land subject to the trust—

(a) if the functions are delegated to him alone, the power is revoked,
(b) if the functions are delegated to him and to other beneficiaries to be exercised by them jointly (but not separately), the power is revoked if each of the other beneficiaries ceases to be so entitled (but otherwise functions exercisable in accordance with the power are so exercisable by the remaining beneficiary or beneficiaries), and

(c)   if the functions are delegated to him and to other beneficiaries to be exercised by them separately (or either separately or jointly), the power is revoked in so far as it relates to him.

(5) A delegation under subsection (1) may be for any period or indefinite.

(6) A power of attorney under subsection (1) cannot be an enduring power within the meaning of the Enduring Powers of Attorney Act 1985.

(7) Beneficiaries to whom functions have been delegated under subsection (1) are, in relation to the exercise of the functions, in the same position as trustees (with the same duties and liabilities); but such beneficiaries shall not be regarded as trustees for any other purposes (including, in particular, the purposes of any enactment permitting the delegation of functions by trustees or imposing requirements relating to the payment of capital money).

(8) Where any function has been delegated to a beneficiary or beneficiaries under subsection (1), the trustees are jointly and severally liable for any act or default of the beneficiary, or any of the beneficiaries, in the exercise of the function if, and only if, the trustees did not exercise reasonable care in deciding to delegate the function to the beneficiary or beneficiaries.

(9) Neither this section nor the repeal by this Act of section 29 of the Law of Property Act 1925 (which is superseded by this section) affects the operation after the commencement of this Act of any delegation effected before that commencement.

Explanatory text—See para **5.8**.

These powers are in addition to ss 23 and 25 of the Trustee Act 1925. Section 29 of the LPA 1925 is repealed.

For a definition of beneficiary entitled to an interest in possession see s 22(2), (3). Those interested under pension schemes are excluded because they are not entitled to an interest in possession.

Subsection (1)—The trustees may delegate by power of attorney any of their functions including a power of sale, cf s 29 of the LPA 1925 which is now repealed. Powers cannot be delegated to persons with a monetary interest only (s 22(3)).

The delegation reproduces the effect of a strict settlement to some extent. The beneficiary entitled to an interest in possession cannot, however, demand that legal estate as of right. It is a discretionary power in the hands of the trustees unless the trust instrument stipulates that the powers should be delegated. The beneficiary to whom the powers are delegated will only be acting as an attorney. The power of attorney is revocable.

For a power of attorney delegating functions, see Precedent 3 in Appendix III.

Subsection (2)—A person dealing in good faith with the delegate is protected unless he had knowledge at the time of the transaction that the delegate was not a person to whom delegation could properly be made.

A purchaser from the person dealing with the delegate will obtain a good title if the person makes a statutory declaration that he was in good faith and did not have knowledge of improper delegations. Declaration must be made before or within three months after the completion of the purchase. Cf Powers of Attorney Act 1971, s 5.

For a statutory declaration satisfying the requirements of s 9(2), see Precedent 4 in Appendix III.

Subsection (3)—The power of attorney has to be given by all the trustees. It can therefore be revoked by any one of them. It will not be revoked by the death or retirement of a trustee. It will, however, be revoked by the appointment of a new trustee as he will not have authorised the delegation. There can, of course, be a fresh delegation.

A power of attorney *expressed* to be irrevocable and given by way of security will not be revocable. As with s 4 of the Powers of Attorney Act 1971, the emphasis is on what is expressed, rather than the actual facts.

Subsection (4)—In order to be a valid delegation the beneficiary must be beneficially entitled to an interest in possession. If he ceases to be so entitled, the delegation to him will be revoked. Where the delegation is to more than one beneficiary, as long as the other(s) remain beneficially entitled to an interest in possession, the delegation to them will remain effective.

Subsection (5)—The delegation need not be limited in time. Cf Trustee Act 1925, s 25 which remains in force. This enables a trustee to delegate his own functions which is not possible under the 1996 Act. A trustee will still be able to employ agents under the Trustee Act 1925, s 23.

Subsection (6)—The essence of delegation under the 1996 Act is that it should be revocable (except where expressed to be given by way of security). Therefore, it cannot be an enduring power of attorney. Delegation under the Trustee Act 1925, s 25 cannot be by enduring power of attorney.

Subsection (7)—As far as the delegated functions are concerned, the beneficiaries have the same liabilities and duties as trustees. However, they are not in the position of trustees for other purposes. They cannot receive capital money and so overreach the equitable interests under the trust. Nor can they sub-delegate their functions.

Subsection (8)—In order not to discourage delegation, the liability of trustees for the acts or default of the beneficiary arises only if they did not exercise reasonable care in deciding to delegate their functions to the beneficiaries. Cf the Trustee Act 1925, s 25.

Subsection (9)—Any pre-commencement delegation under the now repealed Law of Property Act 1925, s 29 will remain effective. Those persons with delegated powers will still continue to operate under s 29.

Consents and consultation

10 Consents

(1) If a disposition creating a trust of land requires the consent of more than two persons to the exercise by the trustees of any function relating to the land, the consent of any two of them to the exercise of the function is sufficient in favour of a purchaser.

(2) Subsection (1) does not apply to the exercise of a function by trustees of land held on charitable, ecclesiastical or public trusts.

(3) Where at any time a person whose consent is expressed by a disposition creating a trust of land to be required to the exercise by the trustees of any function relating to the land is not of full age—

   (a) his consent is not, in favour of a purchaser, required to the exercise of the function, but
   (b) the trustees shall obtain the consent of a parent who has parental responsibility for him (within the meaning of the Children Act 1989) or of a guardian of his.

Explanatory text—See paras **8.3** and **8.4**.

This is derived from the LPA 1925, s 26 which is repealed.

Subsection (1)—This protects a purchaser but not the trustees. They will still be liable if they do not obtain all the specified consents. An application may be made to the court under s 14 to dispense with the need for consents.

Subsection (2)—This is derived from the Settled Land Act 1925, s 29(1). A purchaser who has notice that the land is held on such trusts must satisfy himself that all the necessary consents have been obtained.

Subsection (3)—This is derived from the LPA 1925, s 26(2). The term 'parent who has parental responsibility' is used to make the Act consistent with the LPA 1925. A statutory reference to a parent in a statute passed before the Family Law Reform Act 1987 does not include an unmarried father. An unmarried father does not automatically have responsibility under the Children Act 1989. He will be able to consent on behalf of a minor only if there is a court order or with agreement of the mother.

11 Consultation with beneficiaries

(1) The trustees of land shall in the exercise of any function relating to land subject to the trust—

(a) so far as practicable, consult the beneficiaries of full age and beneficially entitled to an interest in possession in the land, and

(b) so far as consistent with the general interest of the trust, give effect to the wishes of those beneficiaries, or (in case of dispute) of the majority (according to the value of their combined interests).

(2) Subsection (1) does not apply—

(a) in relation to a trust created by a disposition in so far as provision that it does not apply is made by the disposition,

(b) in relation to a trust created or arising under a will made before the commencement of this Act, or

(c) in relation to the exercise of the power mentioned in section 6(2).

(3) Subsection (1) does not apply to a trust created before the commencement of this Act by a disposition, or a trust created after that commencement by reference to such a trust, unless provision to the effect that it is to apply is made by a deed executed—

(a) in a case in which the trust was created by one person and he is of full capacity, by that person, or

(b) in a case in which the trust was created by more than one person, by such of the persons who created the trust as are alive and of full capacity.

(4) A deed executed for the purposes of subsection (3) is irrevocable.

Explanatory text—See paras **5.7.5** and **8.3.2**.

This is derived from the LPA 1925, s 26(3).

Subsection (1)—The reference is to an interest in land because the doctrine of conversion is abolished (s 3).

Subsection (2)—The need to consult can be excluded. This reverses the position under s 26(3) of the LPA 1925 where there was no duty to consult in an express trust for sale if the trust instrument did not so stipulate. Consultation does not apply to a trust created or arising under a will made before the commencement of the Act as a testator would not have envisaged consultation taking place. Nor does it apply to the trustees' power to convey trust land to beneficiaries. The policy of the Act is to allow the trustees to discharge themselves from a trust which no longer serves a useful purpose notwithstanding the views of the beneficiaries.

For a clause excluding or restricting the obligation to consult beneficiaries, see Precedent 12.4 in Appendix III.

Subsection (3)—The duty to consult does not apply to trusts existing before the commencement of the Act unless a deed is executed opting-in to the provisions. For such a deed, see Precedent 5 in Appendix III.

Right of beneficiaries to occupy trust land

12 The right to occupy

(1) A beneficiary who is beneficially entitled to an interest in possession in land subject to a trust of land is entitled by reason of his interest to occupy the land at any time if at that time—

(a) the purposes of the trust include making the land available for his occupation (or for the occupation of beneficiaries of a class of which he is a member or of beneficiaries in general), or

(b) the land is held by the trustees so as to be so available.

(2) Subsection (1) does not confer on a beneficiary a right to occupy land if it is either unavailable or unsuitable for occupation by him.

(3) This section is subject to section 13.

Explanatory text—See para **7.5**.

Subsection (1)—For a definition of beneficially entitled see s 22(2). It was not clear under the legislation before the 1996 Act whether a beneficiary had a right to occupy the land. Compare *Barclay v Barclay* [1970] 2 QB, 677 with *Bull v Bull* [1955] 1 QB, 234. The purposes of the trust must include making the land available for occupation or the land must be held so as to be available. It does not have to have been originally acquired for occupation.

Subsection (2)—There may be cases where although the land is available it is unsuitable for occupancy.

13 Exclusion and restriction of right to occupy

(1) Where two or more beneficiaries are (or apart from this subsection would be) entitled under section 12 to occupy land, the trustees of land may exclude or restrict the entitlement of any one or more (but not all) of them.

(2) Trustees may not under subsection (1)—

(a) unreasonably exclude any beneficiary's entitlement to occupy land, or

(b) restrict any such entitlement to an unreasonable extent.

(3) The trustees of land may from time to time impose reasonable conditions on any beneficiary in relation to his occupation of land by reason of his entitlement under section 12.

(4) The matters to which trustees are to have regard in exercising the powers conferred by this section include—

(a) the intentions of the person or persons (if any) who created the trust,

   (b)   the purposes for which the land is held, and

   (c)   the circumstances and wishes of each of the beneficiaries who is (or apart from any previous exercise by the trustees of those powers would be) entitled to occupy the land under section 12.

(5) The conditions which may be imposed on a beneficiary under subsection (3) include, in particular, conditions requiring him—

   (a)   to pay any outgoings or expenses in respect of the land, or

   (b)   to assume any other obligation in relation to the land or to any activity which is or is proposed to be conducted there.

(6) Where the entitlement of any beneficiary to occupy land under section 12 has been excluded or restricted, the conditions which may be imposed on any other beneficiary under subsection (3) include, in particular, conditions requiring him to—

   (a)   make payments by way of compensation to the beneficiary whose entitlement has been excluded or restricted, or

   (b)   forgo any payment or other benefit to which he would otherwise be entitled under the trust so as to benefit that beneficiary.

(7) The powers conferred on trustees by this section may not be exercised—

   (a)   so as to prevent any person who is in occupation of land (whether or not by reason of an entitlement under section 12) from continuing to occupy the land, or

   (b)   in a manner likely to result in any such person ceasing to occupy the land,

unless he consents or the court has given approval.

(8) The matters to which the court is to have regard in determining whether to give approval under subsection (7) include the matters mentioned in subsection (4)(a) to (c).

Explanatory text—See para **7.5**.

Subsection (1)—Trustees cannot restrict the right of occupation of all the beneficiaries. For a clause where the settlor excludes or restricts the beneficiaries' right to occupy land, see Precedent 12.5 in Appendix III.

Subsection (2)—There is a test of reasonableness on the trustees' exercise of their right to restrict or exclude occupation.

Subsection (3)—The section can apply where only one beneficiary has a right to occupy. The conditions do not have to be imposed at the outset.

Subsection (4)—The list is not exhaustive.

Subsection (5)—The list is not exhaustive. Examples of outgoings or expenses: routine maintenance, water rates. Examples of obligations: ensuring compliance with licensing or planning requirements, or that the property is suitably equipped or furnished.

Subsection (6)—The conditions, again not exhaustive, are directed towards compensating the other beneficiaries for the exclusion or restriction of their right to occupy land.

Subsection (7)—Trustees cannot deprive a person of his occupation unless he consents or the court has given approval. The court means the High Court or a county court (s 23(3)).

Powers of court

14 Applications for order

(1) Any person who is a trustee of land or has an interest in property subject to a trust of land may make an application to the court for an order under this section.

(2) On an application for an order under this section the court may make any such order—

    (a)   relating to the exercise by the trustees of any of their functions (including an order relieving them of any obligation to obtain the consent of, or to consult, any person in connection with the exercise of any of their functions), or

    (b)   declaring the nature or extent of a person's interest in property subject to the trust,

as the court thinks fit.

(3) The court may not under this section make any order as to the appointment or removal of trustees.

(4) The powers conferred on the court by this section are exercisable on an application whether it is made before or after the commencement of this Act.

Explanatory text—See **Ch 6**.

This replaces s 30 of the LPA 1925.

Subsection (1)—Trustees and beneficiaries can apply to the court. The court means the High Court or a county court (s 23(3)). A person who has an interest merely in the personal property of a mixed trust may apply (see definition of 'trust of land' in s 1). So may a person interested in a trust of the proceeds of sale of land (s 17(2)).

Subsection (2)—This confers wider and more flexible powers on the court than under s 30 of the Law of Property Act 1925.

Subsection (3)—Orders for the appointment and removal of trustees must be made under ss 19–21 or under the Trustee Act 1925.

Subsection (4)—Any application under s 30 of the LPA 1925 which have not been dealt with at the time of the commencement of the Act can be dealt with under the new powers in s 14.

15 Matters relevant in determining applications

(1) The matters to which the court is to have regard in determining an application for an order under section 14 include—

    (a)   the intentions of the person or persons (if any) who created the trust,

    (b)   the purposes for which the property subject to the trust is held,

    (c)   the welfare of any minor who occupies or might reasonably be expected to occupy any land subject to the trust as his home, and

    (d)   the interests of any secured creditor of any beneficiary.

(2) In the case of an application relating to the exercise in relation to any land of the powers conferred on the trustees by section 13, the matters to which the court is to have regard also include the circumstances and wishes of each of the beneficiaries

who is (or apart from any previous exercise by the trustees of those powers would be) entitled to occupy the land under section 12.

(3) In the case of any other application, other than one relating to the exercise of the power mentioned in section 6(2), the matters to which the court is to have regard also include the circumstances and wishes of any beneficiaries of full age and entitled to an interest in possession in property subject to the trust or (in case of dispute) of the majority (according to the value of their combined interests).

(4) This section does not apply to an application if section 335A of the Insolvency Act 1986 (which is inserted by Schedule 3 and relates to applications by a trustee of a bankrupt) applies to it.

Explanatory text—See **Ch 6**.

Subsection (1)—The list is not exhaustive. (b) refers to the current purpose under which the land is held rather than the purposes for which it was originally acquired. Cf s 13(4)(a) and (b).

Subsection (2)—Cf s 13(4)(c).

Subsection (3)—Excluded from this requirement is the need to have regard to the wishes of the beneficiaries where the matter relates to the trustees' power to convey the land to beneficiaries of full age who are absolutely entitled. Cf s 11(2)(c).

Subsection (4)—Special rules apply under the Insolvency Act 1986 where an application is made by a trustee in bankruptcy (Sch 3, para 23).

Purchaser protection

16 Protection of purchasers

(1) A purchaser of land which is or has been subject to a trust need not be concerned to see that any requirement imposed on the trustees by section 6(5), 7(3) or 11(1) has been complied with.

(2) Where—

    (a)   trustees of land who convey land which (immediately before it is conveyed) is subject to the trust contravene section 6(6) or (8), but

    (b)   the purchaser of the land from the trustees has no actual notice of the contravention,

the contravention does not invalidate the conveyance.

(3) Where the powers of trustees of land are limited by virtue of section 8—

    (a)   the trustees shall take all reasonable steps to bring the limitation to the notice of any purchaser of the land from them, but

    (b)   the limitation does not invalidate any conveyance by the trustees to a purchaser who has no actual notice of the limitation.

(4) Where trustees of land convey land which (immediately before it is conveyed) is subject to the trust to persons believed by them to be beneficiaries absolutely entitled to the land under the trust and of full age and capacity—

    (a)   the trustees shall execute a deed declaring that they are discharged from the trust in relation to that land, and

    (b)   if they fail to do so, the court may make an order requiring them to do so.

(5) A purchaser of land to which a deed under subsection (4) relates is entitled to assume that, as from the date of the deed, the land is not subject to the trust unless he has actual notice that the trustees were mistaken in their belief that the land was conveyed to beneficiaries absolutely entitled to the land under the trust and of full age and capacity.

(6) Subsections (2) and (3) do not apply to land held on charitable, ecclesiastical or public trusts.

(7) This section does not apply to registered land.

Explanatory text—See **Ch 8**.

The section applies to unregistered title.

Subsection (1)—A purchaser is not concerned to see whether the trustees in exercising their power have:

(1) had regard to the rights of the beneficiaries (s 6(5));
(2) obtained the consent of the beneficiaries before partitioning the land (s 7(3)); and
(3) consulted the beneficiaries and given effect to their wishes (s 11(1)).

Subsection (2)—A conveyance to a purchaser without actual notice of the trustees acting in contravention of any other enactment or rule of law or order or in contravention of a limitation on powers contained in another enactment, will be valid. The beneficiaries may have a claim against the trustees.

Subsection (3)—Where the trustees' powers are limited by the disposition which creates the trust, a purchaser without knowledge of the limitation can rely on the conveyance. Trustees are under a duty to bring the limitation to the notice of a purchaser.

Subsection (4)—This applies where trustees convey the land to beneficiaries they believe are absolutely entitled (either under s 6(2) or in response to a request by the beneficiaries). They must execute a deed of discharge. The court may order them to do so. For a deed of discharge, see Precedent 6 in Appendix III.

Subsection (5)—The deed of discharge protects a purchaser unless he has actual notice that the trustees were wrong.

Subsection (6)—Sections 37 and 39 of the Charities Act 1993 must be satisfied. If not, a purchaser must see that the necessary consents have been obtained (Sch 1, para 4).

Subsection (7)—Where the land is registered, a restriction should be entered on the register if there is any limitation on the trustees' powers. The beneficiaries as well as the trustees can apply for a restriction. The Registrar can rely on a deed of discharge unless he has actual notice that the trustees have made a mistake (Sch 3, para 5(8)).

Supplementary

17 Application of provisions to trusts of proceeds of sale

(1) Section 6(3) applies in relation to trustees of a trust of proceeds of sale of land as in relation to trustees of land.

(2) Section 14 applies in relation to a trust of proceeds of sale of land and trustees of such a trust as in relation to a trust of land and trustees of land.

(3) In this section 'trust of proceeds of sale of land' means (subject to subsection (5)) any trust of property (other than a trust of land) which consists of or includes—

(a) any proceeds of a disposition of land held in trust (including settled land), or

(b) any property representing any such proceeds.

(4) The references in subsection (3) to a trust—

(a) are to any description of trust (whether express, implied, resulting or constructive), including a trust for sale and a bare trust, and
(b) include a trust created, or arising, before the commencement of this Act.

(5) A trust which (despite section 2) is a settlement for the purposes of the Settled Land Act 1925 cannot be a trust of proceeds of sale of land.

(6) In subsection (3)—

(a) 'disposition' includes any disposition made, or coming into operation, before the commencement of this Act, and
(b) the reference to settled land includes personal chattels to which section 67(1) of the Settled Land Act 1925 (heirlooms) applies.

Explanatory text—See para **5.4 and Ch 6**.

Subsection (1)—As trustees of the proceeds of sale of land may purchase land in England and Wales, the power to purchase land is not dependent on there currently being land held in the trusts.

Subsection (2)—The court has power to make orders on applications in relation to trusts of the proceeds of sale of land.

Subsection (3)—'Trusts of land' in s 1 is not defined to include trusts of the proceeds of sale of land and so trusts of the proceeds of sale of land need a separate definition. It is only relevant for ss 6(3) and 14. Trust of the proceeds includes money representing the sale of land held under: a trust for sale; a trust of land; a former strict settlement; a bare trust; and any property other than land in which that money is invested. A trust is defined in the same terms as s 1(2)(a).

Subsection (5)—A trust of the proceeds of sale of land will only arise where a settlement for the purposes of the Settled Land Act 1925 no longer exists. If settled land is sold but the settlement still contains other land or heirlooms, the proceeds of sale will be part of the settlement and not a trust of the proceeds of the sale of land.

Subsection (6)—If land subject to a trust for sale was sold before the Act came into force, any proceeds of the sale of the land still held by the trustees will be held on a trust of the proceeds of sale. Land which was settled under s 17(3)(a) includes heirlooms. See definition of 'relevant property' in s 2(4).

18 Application of Part to personal representatives

(1) The provisions of this Part relating to trustees, other than sections 10, 11 and 14, apply to personal representatives, but with appropriate modifications and without prejudice to the functions of personal representatives for the purposes of administration.

(2) The appropriate modifications include—

(a) the substitution of references to persons interested in the due administration of the estate for references to beneficiaries, and
(b) the substitution of references to the will for references to the disposition creating the trust.

(3) Section 3(1) does not apply to personal representatives if the death occurs before the commencement of this Act.

Explanatory text—See para **5.9**.

Subsection (1)—Personal representatives are given the powers of trustees but they are not subject to the provisions relating to consents and consultations. Nor can they make an application to the court for an order under s 14. The policy of the Act is that trusts of land which arise on death should be similar in nature to inter vivos trusts. Unless the administration of the deceased's estate has been completed, personal representatives are not trustees; hence the need for the section.

Subsection (2)—The modifications are not exhaustive. Those entitled under a will are not beneficiaries before the administration is complete but only persons interested in the due administration of the estate.

Subsection (3)—The doctrine of conversion will continue to apply if the deceased died before the commencement of the Act. Therefore, if personal representatives were treating land under a trust for sale as personal property, they will continue to do so.

PART II
APPOINTMENT AND RETIREMENT OF TRUSTEES

19 Appointment and retirement of trustee at instance of beneficiaries

(1) This section applies in the case of a trust where—

  (a)   there is no person nominated for the purpose of appointing new trustees by the instrument, if any, creating the trust, and

  (b)   the beneficiaries under the trust are of full age and capacity and (taken together) are absolutely entitled to the property subject to the trust.

(2) The beneficiaries may give a direction or directions of either or both of the following descriptions—

  (a)   a written direction to a trustee or trustees to retire from the trust, and

  (b)   a written direction to the trustees or trustee for the time being (or, if there are none, to the personal representative of the last person who was a trustee) to appoint by writing to be a trustee or trustees the person or persons specified in the direction.

(3) Where—

  (a)   a trustee has been given a direction under subsection (2)(a),

  (b)   reasonable arrangements have been made for the protection of any rights of his in connection with the trust,

  (c)   after he has retired there will be either a trust corporation or at least two persons to act as trustees to perform the trust, and

  (d)   either another person is to be appointed to be a new trustee on his retirement (whether in compliance with a direction under subsection (2)(b) or otherwise) or the continuing trustees by deed consent to his retirement,

he shall make a deed declaring his retirement and shall be deemed to have retired and be discharged from the trust.

(4) Where a trustee retires under subsection (3) he and the continuing trustees (together with any new trustee) shall (subject to any arrangements for the protection of his rights) do anything necessary to vest the trust property in the continuing trustees (or the continuing and new trustees).

(5) This section has effect subject to the restrictions imposed by the Trustee Act 1925 on the number of trustees.

Explanatory text—See **Ch 4**.

The section applies to trusts of personal property as well as land.

Subsection (1)—The beneficiaries must be in a position to terminate the trust under the rule in *Saunders v Vautier* (1841) 4 Beav 115. The effect of the section is to reverse the decision in *Re Brockbank* [1948] Ch 206. The beneficiaries' right arises only if no one is nominated in the trust instrument to make the appointment. It takes priority over the right of the surviving or continuing trustees under s 36(1)(b) and (6)(b) of the Trustee Act 1925.

Subsection (2)—As originally drafted, the Bill only referred to the appointment, not the retirement of trustees. For a form of directions by beneficiaries for the appointment or retirement of trustees, see Precedent 7 in Appendix III.

Subsection (3)—Arrangements for the protection of the retiring trustee should be implemented no later than the date when the actual retirement takes place. The retiring trustee has the ability to defer executing the deeds until reasonable arrangements have been made.

For a deed of retirement, see Precedent 9 in Appendix III.

Subsection (4)—The deed of retirement should contain a declaration by the retiring and continuing trustees vesting the property in the continuing trustees. One will be implied unless there is a contrary intention. Mortgages, leases with a covenant against assignment and stocks and shares will have to be transferred separately (Trustee Act 1925, s 40(2), (3)).

Subsection (5)—Trustees of a trust of land are limited to four (Trustee Act 1925, s 34).

20 Appointment of substitute for incapable trustee

(1) This section applies where—

    (a)   a trustee is incapable by reason of mental disorder of exercising his functions as trustee,

    (b)   there is no person who is both entitled and willing and able to appoint a trustee in place of him under section 36(1) of the Trustee Act 1925, and

    (c)   the beneficiaries under the trust are of full age and capacity and (taken together) are absolutely entitled to the property subject to the trust.

(2) The beneficiaries may give to—

    (a)   a receiver of the trustee,

    (b)   an attorney acting for him under the authority of a power of attorney created by an instrument which is registered under section 6 of the Enduring Powers of Attorney Act 1985, or

    (c)   a person authorised for the purpose by the authority having jurisdiction under Part VII of the Mental Health Act 1983,

a written direction to appoint by writing the person or persons specified in the direction to be a trustee or trustees in place of the incapable trustee.

Explanatory text—See para **4.6**.

Subsection (1)—The beneficiaries' right will arise only if those persons nominated in the trust instrument or the surviving and continuing trustees or the personal representatives of the last surviving or continuing trustees do not want to make the appointment. If the appointment by the receiver were against the wishes of the continuing trustees, there would be problems about the vesting of the property in the new trustee.

Subsection (2)—The direction and the appointment must be in writing. For a form of directions, see Precedent 8 in Appendix III.

21 Supplementary

(1) For the purposes of section 19 or 20 a direction is given by beneficiaries if—

(a)   a single direction is jointly given by all of them, or
(b)   (subject to subsection (2)) a direction is given by each of them (whether solely or jointly with one or more, but not all, of the others),

and none of them by writing withdraws the direction given by him before it has been complied with.

(2) Where more than one direction is given each must specify for appointment or retirement the same person or persons.

(3) Subsection (7) of section 36 of the Trustee Act 1925 (powers of trustees appointed under that section) applies to a trustee appointed under section 19 or 20 as if he were appointed under that section.

(4) A direction under section 19 or 20 must not specify a person or persons for appointment if the appointment of that person or those persons would be in contravention of section 35(1) of the Trustee Act 1925 or section 24(1) of the Law of Property Act 1925 (requirements as to identity of trustees).

(5) Sections 19 and 20 do not apply in relation to a trust created by a disposition in so far as provision that they do not apply is made by the disposition.

(6) Sections 19 and 20 do not apply in relation to a trust created before the commencement of this Act by a disposition in so far as provision to the effect that they do not apply is made by a deed executed—

(a)   in a case in which the trust was created by one person and he is of full capacity, by that person, or
(b)   in a case in which the trust was created by more than one person, by such of the persons who created the trust as are alive and of full capacity.

(7) A deed executed for the purposes of subsection (6) is irrevocable.

(8) Where a deed is executed for the purposes of subsection (6)—

(a)   it does not affect anything done before its execution to comply with a direction under section 19 or 20, but
(b)   a direction under section 19 or 20 which has been given but not complied with before its execution shall cease to have effect.

Explanatory text—See **Ch 4**.

Subsection (1)—The direction must be unanimous, although for convenience it is possible for the beneficiaries to give separate directions. A beneficiary is entitled to withdraw his direction before it is complied with. He may have been subject to undue influence. For a form of withdrawal of direction, see Precedent 10 in Appendix III.

Subsection (2)—Failure to specify the same person will mean that the direction is not unanimous and so it will be ineffective.

Subsection (3)—Express provision that s 36(7) of the Trustee Act 1925 is to apply is necessary because the appointment is not made under s 36 of that Act. It is not made by persons empowered under that Act to appoint new trustees. Section 36(7) provides that a new trustee will have the same powers as if he had originally been appointed a trustee by the trust instrument.

Subsection (4)—The same persons must be appointed trustees of the land and the proceeds of sale (even though the appointments must be made by separate instruments).

Subsection (5)—It is possible for the creation of the trust to provide that the beneficiaries shall not have power to direct the appointment and/or retirement of trustees. For such a clause, see Precedent 12.6 in Appendix III.

Subsections (6), (7) and (8)—The power of the beneficiaries to give directions applies to trusts created before the commencement of the Act (as well as after). However, it is possible to opt out if the creator of the trust, or the surviving creators, execute a deed to that effect. A precedent for such a deed appears as Precedent 11 in Appendix III.

PART III
SUPPLEMENTARY

22 Meaning of 'beneficiary'

(1) In this Act 'beneficiary', in relation to a trust, means any person who under the trust has an interest in property subject to the trust (including a person who has such an interest as a trustee or a personal representative).

(2) In this Act references to a beneficiary who is beneficially entitled do not include a beneficiary who has an interest in property subject to the trust only by reason of being a trustee or personal representative.

(3) For the purposes of this Act a person who is a beneficiary only by reason of being an annuitant is not to be regarded as entitled to an interest in possession in land subject to the trust.

Explanatory text—See para **7.1.**

Subsection (1)—Beneficiary includes those whose interest in the trust is of a fiduciary nature and also persons whose interest in a mixed trust of land and personalty is an interest in the personalty only.

Subsection (2)—Trustees and personal representatives are excluded from the term beneficially entitled (s 9 (delegation), ss 12 and 13 (right to occupy land)).

Subsection (3)—A beneficiary entitled to an interest in possession does not include an annuitant.

23 Other interpretation provisions

(1) In this Act 'purchaser' has the same meaning as in Part I of the Law of Property Act 1925.

(2) Subject to that, where an expression used in this Act is given a meaning by the Law of Property Act 1925 it has the same meaning as in that Act unless the context otherwise requires.

(3) In this Act 'the court' means—

    (a)   the High Court, or
    (b)   a county court.

Subsection (1)—Purchaser means a person who acquires an interest in or charge on property for money or money's worth.

Subsection (2)—The Law of Property Act 1925, s 205 is the definition section.

Subsection (3)—Under the High Court and County Court Jurisdiction Order 1991, Art 2, para 1(a), county courts are given jurisdiction under s 30 of the Law of Property Act 1925 'whatever the amount involved in the proceeds and whatever the value of any fund or asset connected with the proceedings'. The jurisdiction is concurrent with that of the High Court. The position is the same under s 14 of the 1996 Act.

24 Application to Crown

(1) Subject to subsection (2), this Act binds the Crown.

(2) This Act (except so far as it relates to undivided shares and joint ownership) does not affect or alter the descent, devolution or nature of the estates and interests of or in—

 (a) land for the time being vested in Her Majesty in right of the Crown or of the Duchy of Lancaster, or
 (b) land for the time being belonging to the Duchy of Cornwall and held in right or respect of the Duchy.

Subsections (1) and (2)—The Act, like the Law of Property Act 1925 and the Trustee Act 1925, binds the Crown but excludes land belonging to the Duchy of Lancaster and the Duchy of Cornwall.

25 Amendments, repeals etc.

(1) The enactments mentioned in Schedule 3 have effect subject to the amendments specified in that Schedule (which are minor or consequential on other provisions of this Act).

(2) The enactments mentioned in Schedule 4 are repealed to the extent specified in the third column of that Schedule.

(3) Neither section 2(5) nor the repeal by this Act of section 29 of the Settled Land Act 1925 applies in relation to the deed of settlement set out in the Schedule to the Chequers Estate Act 1917 or the trust instrument set out in the Schedule to the Chevening Estate Act 1959.

(4) The amendments and repeals made by this Act do not affect any entailed interest created before the commencement of this Act.

(5) The amendments and repeals made by this Act in consequence of section 3—

 (a) do not affect a trust created by a will if the testator died before the commencement of this Act, and
 (b) do not affect personal representatives of a person who died before that commencement;

and the repeal of section 22 of the Partnership Act 1890 does not apply in any circumstances involving the personal representatives of a partner who died before that commencement.

Subsections (1) and (2)—Subject to subsections (3) and (4) the amendments and repeals in Schs 3 and 4 will apply to all trusts and settlements whether created before or after commencement of the Act.

Subsection (3)—Land under these Acts will continue to be governed by the Settled Land Act 1925.

Subsection (4)—Existing entails will continue. Parliament has created by statute unbarrable entails which still exist, 3 & 4 Anne, c 6 (1704); 5 Anne, c 3 (1706) (Duke of Marlborough); 54 Geo 3, c 161 (1814) (Duke of Wellington).

Subsection (5)—The abolition of the doctrine of conversion does not affect a trust created by a will if the testator died before the commencement of the Act. Nor does it affect the personal representatives of a person who died before the commencement.

Under s 22 of the Partnership Act 1890, where land has become partnership property it is treated as between the partners and their personal representatives as personal property unless there is a contrary intention. The position is preserved for personal representatives of a partner who died before the commencement of the Act, as the testator would not have had an opportunity to reconsider the effect of the new law.

26 Power to make consequential provision

(1) The Lord Chancellor may by order made by statutory instrument make any such supplementary, transitional or incidental provision as appears to him to be appropriate for any of the purposes of this Act or in consequence of any of the provisions of this Act.

(2) An order under subsection (1) may, in particular, include provision modifying any enactment contained in a public general or local Act which is passed before, or in the same Session as, this Act.

(3) A statutory instrument made in the exercise of the power conferred by this section is subject to annulment in pursuance of a resolution of either House of Parliament.

Subsections (1) and (2)—The purpose of these provisions is to cover unforeseen circumstances where the existing law concerning strict settlements and trusts for sale would apply. Also there might have been other Bills passed in the same session which assume that the existing law relating to trusts still applied. Such an Act might have to be subsequently amended.

Subsection (3)—Any statutory instrument made under subsections 1 and 2 is subject to the negative resolution procedure under s 5(1) of the Statutory Instruments Act 1946. This level of security is considered appropriate as the power is available only to the supplementary, transitional or incidental purposes of the Act.

27 Short title, commencement and extent

(1) This Act may be cited as the Trusts of Land and Appointment of Trustees Act 1996.

(2) This Act comes into force on such day as the Lord Chancellor appoints by order made by statutory instrument.

(3) Subject to subsection (4), the provisions of this Act extend only to England and Wales.

(4) The repeal in section 30(2) of the Agriculture Act 1970 extends only to Northern Ireland.

Subsection (1)—The title does not reflect the fact that the Act also provides for the retirement of trustees. The ability for beneficiaries to direct the retirement of trustees was added during the passage of the Bill in the House of Lords.

Subsection (2)—It is considered that some time is needed for practitioners to adjust to the new legislation.

Subsections (3) and (4)—The Act applies to England and Wales. Section 30(2) of the Agriculture Act 1970 makes reference to the provisions of the Law of Property Act 1925, and covers Northern Ireland only.

SCHEDULES

SCHEDULE 1
PROVISIONS CONSEQUENTIAL ON SECTION 2

Section 2

Minors

1 (1) Where after the commencement of this Act a person purports to convey a legal estate in land to a minor, or two or more minors, alone, the conveyance—

    (a)   is not effective to pass the legal estate, but

    (b)   operates as a declaration that the land is held in trust for the minor or minors (or if he purports to convey it to the minor or minors in trust for any persons, for those persons).

(2) Where after the commencement of this Act a person purports to convey a legal estate in land to—

    (a)   a minor or two or more minors, and

    (b)   another person who is, or other persons who are, of full age,

the conveyance operates to vest the land in the other person or persons in trust for the minor or minors and the other person or persons (or if he purports to convey it to them in trust for any persons, for those persons).

(3) Where immediately before the commencement of this Act a conveyance is operating (by virtue of section 27 of the Settled Land Act 1925) as an agreement to execute a settlement in favour of a minor or minors—

    (a)   the agreement ceases to have effect on the commencement of this Act, and

    (b)   the conveyance subsequently operates instead as a declaration that the land is held in trust for the minor or minors.

2 Where after the commencement of this Act a legal estate in land would, by reason of intestacy or in any other circumtances not dealt with in paragraph 1, vest in a person who is a minor if he were a person of full age, the land is held in trust for the minor.

Family charges

3 Where, by virtue of an instrument coming into operation after the commencement of this Act, land becomes charged voluntarily (or in consideration of marriage) or by way of family arrangement, whether immediately or after an interval, with the payment of—

    (a)   a rentcharge for the life of a person or a shorter period, or

    (b)   capital, annual or periodical sums for the benefit of a person,

the instrument operates as a declaration that the land is held in trust for giving effect to the charge.

Charitable, ecclesiastical and public trusts

4   (1) This paragraph applies in the case of land held on charitable, ecclesiastical or public trusts (other than land to which the Universities and College Estates Act 1925 applies).

(2) Where there is a conveyance of such land—

(a)   if neither section 37(1) nor section 39(1) of the Charities Act 1993 applies to the conveyance, it shall state that the land is held on such trusts, and

(b)   if neither section 37(2) nor section 39(2) of that Act has been complied with in relation to the conveyance and a purchaser has notice that the land is held on such trusts, he must see that any consents or orders necesssary to authorise the transaction have been obtained.

(3) Where any trustees or the majority of any set of trustees have power to transfer or create any legal estate in the land, the estate shall be transferred or created by them in the names and on behalf of the persons in whom it is vested.

Entailed interests

5   (1) Where a person purports by an instrument coming into operation after the commencement of this Act to grant to another person an entailed interest in real or personal property, the instrument—

(a)   is not effective to grant an entailed interest, but

(b)   operates instead as a declaration that the property is held in trust absolutely for the person to whom an entailed interest in the property was purportedly granted.

(2) Where a person purports by an instrument coming into operation after the commencement of this Act to declare himself a tenant in tail or real or personal property, the instrument is not effective to create an entailed interest.

Property held on settlement ceasing to exist

6   Where a settlement ceases to be a settlement for the purposes of the Settled Land Act 1925 because no relevant property (within the meaning of section 2(4)) is, or is deemed to be, subject to the settlement, any property which is or later becomes subject to the settlement is held in trust for the persons interested under the settlement.

Paragraph 1—This replaces the Law of Property Act 1925, s 19. A purported conveyance to a minor operates as a trust of land for the minor.

Paragraph 1(1)(b)—The conveyance is the document for the purposes of s 53(1)(b) of the Law of Property Act 1925. Conveyances to minors as joint tenants or tenants in common are included.

Paragraph 1(2)—The conveyance is effective to pass the legal estate which is held on trust for the adult(s) and minor(s).

Paragraph 1(3)—Section 2(1) prevents the creation of new strict settlements. Agreements under s 27 of the Settled Land Act 1925 which are subsisting at the commencement of the Act will cease. The subsequent conveyance operates as declaration of trust.

Paragraph 2—If for any other reason land would vest in a minor, eg on intestacy land is held on trust for the minor.

Paragraph 3—Section 1(1)(v) of the Settled Land Act 1925 provides that family charges will create a settlement. After the commencement of the Act, an instrument making such a charge will operate as a declaration of trust to give effect to the charge. Any trustee in whom the land is vested may sell the land subject to the charge or appoint another trustee and overreach the charge. The reference to a declaration of trust ensures compliance with s 53(1)(b) of the LPA 1925.

Paragraph 4(1)—Such trusts will no longer be deemed to be strict settlements but will be trusts of land.

Paragraph 4(2)—If ss 37 and 39 of the Charities Act 1993 do not apply, the purchasers continue to be in the same position as they were under s 29 of the Settled Land Act 1925. The conveyance must state that the land is held on charitable, ecclesiastical or public trusts. Any purchaser with notice must see that any necessary consents or orders have been obtained.

Under the Charities Act 1993, s 36(1), charitable land may not be disposed of without an order of the court or the Charity Commissioners. Not only conveyances but other instruments including contracts for the disposition of land must state that the land is held on charitable, ecclesiastical or public trusts (s 37(1)). It is for the trustees to ensure and certify that all the necessary consents and orders have been obtained (s 37(2)). Where land is registered, a restriction must be entered on the register preventing any disposition taking place unless there is compliance with the restrictions on the disposition of charitable land (s 37(3)).

Paragraph 5—Section 130(1), (3) and (6) of the LPA 1925 is repealed. An interest purporting to grant a person an entailed interest operates as a declaration of trust to hold the property absolutely for that person. If he is of full age he can call for the legal estate under the rule in *Saunders v Vautier* (1841) 4 Beav 115.

If a person declares himself to be a tenant in tail the instrument is ineffective.

Paragraph 6—If a settlement ceases to have any land or heirlooms, any property which later becomes subject to the settlement must be held on trust.

SCHEDULE 2
AMENDMENTS OF STATUTORY PROVISIONS IMPOSING TRUST FOR SALE

Section 5

Mortgaged property held by trustees after redemption barred

1 (1) Section 31 of the Law of Property Act 1925 (implied trust for sale of mortgaged property where right of redemption is barred) is amended as follows.

(2) In subsection (1), for the words 'on trust of sale.' substitute 'in trust—

(a)   to apply the income from the property in the same manner as interest paid on the mortagage debt would have been applicable; and

(b)   if the property is sold, to apply the net proceeds of sale, after payment of costs and expenses, in the same manner as repayment of the mortgage debt would have been applicable.'

(3) In subsection (2), for the words from the beginning to 'this subsection' substitute—

'(2) Subsection (1) of this section'.

(4) Omit subsection (3).

(5) For subsection (4) substitute—

'(4) Where—

    (a)   the mortgage money is capital money for the purposes of the Settled Land Act 1925;

    (b)   land other than any forming the whole or part of the property mentioned in subsection (1) of this section is, or is deemed to be, subject to the settlement; and

    (c)   the tenant for life or statutory owner requires the trustees to execute with respect to land forming the whole or part of that property a vesting deed such as would have been required in relation to the land if it had been acquired on a purchase with capital money,

the trustees shall execute such a vesting deed.'

(6) In accordance with the amendments made by sub-paragraphs (2) to (5), in the sidenote of section 31 for the words 'Trust for sale' substitute 'Trust'.

(7) The amendments made by this paragraph—

    (a)   apply whether the right of redemption is discharged before or after the commencement of this Act, but

    (b)   are without prejudice to any dealings or arrangements made before the commencement of this Act.

Land purchased by trustees of personal property etc.

2   (1) Section 32 of the Law of Property Act 1925 (implied trust for sale of land acquired by trustees of personal property or of land held on trust for sale) is omitted.

(2) The repeal made by this paragraph applies in relation to land purchased after the commencement of this Act whether the trust or will in pursuance of which it is purchased comes into operation before or after the commencement of this Act.

Dispositions to tenants in common

3   (1) Section 34 of the Law of Property Act 1925 is amended as follows.

(2) In subsection (2) (conveyance of land in undivided shares to operate as conveyance to grantees on trust for sale), for the words from 'upon the statutory trusts' to 'those shares' substitute 'in trust for the persons interested in the land'.

(3) In subsection (3) (devise etc. of land in undivided shares to operate as devise etc. to trustees of will etc. on trust for sale)—

    (a)   omit the words from 'the trustees (if any)' to 'then to' and the words 'in each case', and

    (b)   for the words 'upon the statutory trusts hereinafter mentioned' substitute 'in trust for the persons interested in the land'.

(4) After that subsection insert—

'(3A) In subsections (2) and (3) of this section references to the persons interested in the land include persons interested as trustees or personal representatives (as well as persons beneficially interested).'

(5) Omit subsection (4) (settlement of undivided shares in land to operate only as settlement of share of profits of sale and rents and profits).

(6) The amendments made by this paragraph apply whether the disposition is made, or comes into operation, before or after the commencement of this Act.

Joint tenancies

4   (1) Section 36 of the Law of Property Act 1925 is amended as follows.

(2) In subsection (1) (implied trust for sale applicable to land held for persons as joint tenants), for the words 'on trust for sale' substitute 'in trust'.

(3) In subsection (2) (severance of beneficial joint tenancy)—

  (a)   in the proviso, for the words 'under the trust for sale affecting the land the net proceeds of sale, and the net rents and profits until sale, shall be held upon the trust' substitute 'the land shall be held in trust on terms', and
  (b)   in the final sentence, for the words 'on trust for sale' substitute 'in trust'.

(4) The amendments made by this paragraph apply whether the legal estate is limited, or becomes held in trust, before or after the commencement of this Act.

Intestacy

5   (1) Section 33 of the Administration of Estates Act 1925 (implied trust for sale on intestacy) is amended as follows.

(2) For subsection (1) substitute—

  '(1) On the death of a person intestate as to any real or personal estate, that estate shall be held in trust by his personal representatives with the power to sell it.'

(3) In subsection (2), for the words from the beginning to 'pay all' substitute—

  '(2) The personal representatives shall pay out of—

  (a)   the ready money of the deceased (so far as not disposed of by his will, if any); and
  (b)   any set money arising from disposing of any other part of his estate (after payment of costs),

  all'.

(4) In subsection (4), for the words from 'including' to 'retained' substitute 'and any part of the estate of the deceased which remains'.

(5) The amendments made by this paragraph apply whether the death occurs before or after the commencement of this Act.

Reverter of sites

6   (1) Section 1 of the Reverter of Sites Act 1987 (right of reverter replaced by trust for sale) is amended as follows.

  (2) In subsection (2)—

  (a)   after 'a trust' insert 'for the persons who (but for this Act) would from time to time be entitled to the ownership of the land by virtue of its reverter with a power, without consulting them,', and

(b)   for the words 'upon trust' onwards susbtitute 'in trust for those persons; but they shall not be entitled by reason of their interest to occupy the land.'

(3) In subsection (3), for the words 'trustees for sale' substitute 'trustees'.

(4) In subsection (4), for the words 'on trust for sale' substitute 'in trust'.

(5) In accordance with the amendments made by this paragraph, in the sidenote, for 'trust for sale' substitute 'trust'.

(6) The amendments made by this paragraph apply whether the trust arises before or after the commencement of this Act.

Trusts deemed to arise in 1926

7   Where at the commencement of this Act any land is held on trust for sale, or on the statutory trusts, by virtue of Schedule 1 to the Law of Property Act 1925 (transitional provisions), it shall after that commencement be held in trust for the persons interested in the land; and references in that Schedule to trusts for sale or trustees for sale or to the statutory trusts shall be construed accordingly.

Paragraph 1—Section 31 of the LPA 1925 is amended. The changes apply whether the right of redemption is discharged before or after commencement of the Act but they do not affect dealings or arrangements before the Act. The new s 31(4) is confined in its operation to settlements which are able to acquire new settled land after the commencement of the Act. Other new land will be held on a trust of land and the section is therefore inappropriate.

Paragraph 2—This repeals s 32 of the Law of Property Act 1925.

Paragraph 3—This amends s 34 of the LPA 1925.
   A disposition of land to tenants in common will operate as a trust of land, rather than a trust for sale.
   Subparagraph (4) incorporates the definition of persons interested in the trust in s 22(1) into s 34 of the LPA 1925.

Paragraph 4—This amends s 36 of the LPA 1925 to impose a trust rather than a trust for sale. It makes clear that following the abolition of the doctrine of conversion, the interest under the trust is an equitable interest in land rather than the proceeds of sale.

Paragraph 5—This amends s 33 of the Administration of Estates Act 1925.
   Personal representatives will hold land on a trust of land. Sections 6(1) and 18 give personal representatives power to sell land. This paragraph ensures that personal representatives can also sell personal property.

Paragraph 6—Section 1 of the Reverter of Sites Act 1987 provides that where land was given for charitable purposes with provision to revert to the grantor's successors should those purposes fail, the trustees in whom the land was vested should hold the land on trust for sale for the revertee. The trustees will now hold on trust for these persons.

Paragraph 7—This amends Sch 1 to the Law of Property Act 1925 (this contains transitional provisions imposing a statutory trust for sale on interests existing before the commencement of the Act).
   The land will now be held on trust rather than trust for sale.

SCHEDULE 3
MINOR AND CONSEQUENTIAL AMENDMENTS

Section 25(1)

The Law of Property Act 1922 (c 16)

1 In paragraph 17(3) and (4) of Schedule 15 to the Law of Property Act 1922, for the words 'held on trust for sale' substitute 'subject to a trust of land'.

The Settled Land Act 1925 (c 18)

2 (1) The Settled land Act 1925 is amended as follows.

(2) In section 1(1)(ii)(c), after the word 'fee' insert '(other than a fee which is a fee simple absolute by virtue of section 7 of the Law of Property Act 1925)'.

(3) In section 3, for the words 'not held upon trust for sale which has been subject to a settlement' substitute 'which has been subject to a settlement which is a settlement for the purposes of this Act'.

(4) In section 7(5), for the words 'trustee for sale' substitute 'trustee of land'.

(5) In section 12(1), for the words 'trustee for sale' substitute 'trustee of land'.

(6) In section 17—

    (a)   in subsection (1)—
        (i)   for the words 'trust for sale', in the first three places, substitute 'trust of land', and
        (ii) for the words 'held on trust for sale' substitute 'subject to a trust of land',
    (b)   in subsection (2)(c), for the words 'a conveyance on trust for sale' substitute 'land', and
    (c)   in subsection (3), for the words 'any trust for sale' substitute 'a trust of land'.

(7) In section 18(2)(b), for the words 'trustee for sale' substitute 'trustee of land'.

(8) In section 20(1)(viii), for the words 'an immediate binding trust for sale' substitute 'a trust of land'.

(9) In section 30(1)—

    (a)   in paragraph (iii), for the words 'power of or upon trust for sale of' substitute 'a power or duty to sell', and
    (b)   in paragraph (iv)—
        (i)   for the words 'future power of sale, or under a future trust for sale of' substitute 'a future power or duty to sell', and
        (ii) for the words 'or trust' substitute 'or duty'.

(10) In section 33(1), for the words 'any power of sale, or trust for sale' substitute 'a power or duty to sell'.

(11) In section 36—

    (a)   for the words—
        (i)   'upon the statutory trusts' in subsection (2), and

  (ii) 'on the statutory trust' in subsection (3),
  substitute 'in trust for the persons interested in the land',

 (b) in subsection (4), for the words 'trust for sale' substitute 'trust of land',

 (c) for subsection (6) substitute—

  '(6) In subsections (2) and (3) of this section references to the persons interested in the land include persons interested as trustees or personal representatives (as well as persons beneficially interested).', and

 (d) in accordance with the amendments made by paragraphs (a) to (c) in the sidenote, for the words 'trust for sale of the land' substitute 'trust of land'.

(12) In section 110(5), for the words 'trustee for sale' substitute 'trustee of land'.

(13) In section 117(1)—

 (a) in paragraph (ix), for the words 'not being' substitute ', but does not (except in the phrase 'trust of land') include', and

 (b) in paragraph (xxx), for the words ' "trustees for sale" and "power to postpone a sale" have the same meanings' substitute 'has the same meaning'.

The Trustee Act 1925 (c 19)

3 (1) The Trustee Act 1925 is amended as follows.

(2) In section 12—

 (a) in subsection (1), for the words 'a trust for sale or a power of sale of property is vested in a trustee' substitute 'a trustee has a duty or power to sell property', and

 (b) in subsection (2) for the word 'trust', in both places, substitute 'duty'.

(3) In section 14(2), for paragraph (a) substitute—

 '(a) proceeds or sale or other capital money arising under a trust of land;'.

(4) In section 19—

 (a) in subsection (1), for the words 'against loss or damage by fire any building or other insurable property' substitute 'any personal property against loss or damage', and

 (b) in subsection (2), for the words 'building or' substitute 'personal'.

(5) In section 20(3)(c), for the words 'property held upon trust for sale' substitute 'land subject to a trust of land or personal property held on trust for sale'.

(6) In section 24—

 (a) for the words 'the proceeds of sale of land directed to be sold, or in any other' substitute 'any'.

 (b) for the words 'trust for sale' substitute 'trust',

 (c) for the words 'trustees for sale' substitute 'trustees', and

 (d) for the words 'trust or' substitute 'duty or'.

(7) In section 27(1), for the words 'or of a disposition on trust for sale' substitute ', trustees of land, trustees for sale of personal property'.

(8) In section 32, for subsection (2) substitute—

'(2) This section does not apply to capital money arising under the Settled Land Act 1925.'

(9) In section 34(2), for the words 'on trust for sale of land' substitute 'creating trust of land'.

(10) In section 35—

(a)   for subsection (1) substitute—

'(1) Appointments of new trustees of land and of new trustees of any trust of the proceeds of sale of the land shall, subject to any order of the court, be effected by separate instruments, but in such manner as to secure that the same persons become trustees of land and trustees of the trust of the proceeds of sale.',

(b)   for subsection (3) substitute—

'(3) Where new trustees of land are appointed, a memorandum of the persons who are for the time being the trustees of the land shall be endorsed on or annexed to the conveyance by which the land was vested in trustees of land; and that conveyance shall be produced to the persons who are for the time being the trustees of the land by the person in possession of it in order for that to be done when the trustees require its production.', and

(c)   in accordance with the amendments made by paragraphs (a) and (b), in the sidenote, for the words 'dispositions on trust for sale of land' substitute 'and trustees of land'.

(11) In section 36(6), for the words before paragraph (a) substitute—

'(6) Where, in the case of any trust, there are not more than three trustees—'.

(12) In section 37(1)(c), for the word 'individuals' substitute 'persons'.

(13) In section 39(1), for the word 'individuals' substitute 'persons'.

(14) In section 40(2), for the words 'the statutory power' substitute 'section 39 of this Act or section 19 of the Trusts of Land and Appointment of Trustees Act 1996'.

The Law of Property Act 1925 (c 20)

4   (1) The Law of Property Act 1925 is amended as follows.

(2) In section 2—

(a)   in subsection (1), in paragraph (ii)—
    (i)   for the words 'trustees for sale' substitute 'trustees of land', and
    (ii)   for the words 'the statutory requirements respecting the payment of capital money arising under a disposition upon trust for sale' substitute 'the requirements of section 27 of this Act respecting the payment of capital money arising on such a conveyance',
(b)   after that subsection insert—

'(1A) An equitable interest in land subject to a trust of land which remains in, or is to revert to, the settlor shall (subject to any contrary intention) be overreached by the conveyance if it would be so overreached were it an interest under the trust.', and

  (c) in subsection (2)—

    (i)   for the words 'a trust for sale' substitute 'a trust of land',

    (ii)   for the words 'under the trust for sale or the powers conferred on the trustees for sale' substitute 'by the trustees', and

    (iii) for the words 'to the trust for sale' substitute 'to the trust'.

(3) In section 3(1)(c), for the words 'Where the legal estate affected is neither settled land nor vested in trustees for sale' substitute 'In any other case'.

(4) In section 16—

  (a) in subsection (2), for the words 'pursuant to a trust for sale' substitute 'by trustees of land', and

  (b) in subsection (6), for the words 'trustee for sale' substitute 'trustee of land'.

(5) In section 18—

  (a) in subsection (1)—

    (i)   after the word 'settled' insert 'or held subject to a trust of land', and

    (ii)   for the words 'trustee for sale' substitute 'trustee of land', and

  (b) in subsection (2)(b), for the words 'of the land or of the proceeds of sale' substitute 'or trust'.

(6) In section 22(2)—

  (a) for the words 'held on trust for sale' substitute 'subject to a trust of land' and

  (b) for the words 'under the trust for sale or under the powers vested in the trustees for sale' substitute 'by the trustees',

and, in accordance with the amendments made by paragraphs (a) and (b), in the sidenote of section 22, for the words 'on trust for sale' substitute 'in trust'.

(7) For section 24 substitute—

'Trusts of land

24 Appointment of trustees of land

(1) The persons having power to appoint new trustees of land shall be bound to appoint the same persons (if any) who are for the time being trustees of any trust of the proceeds of sale of the land.

(2) A purchaser shall not be concerned to see that subsection (1) of this section has been complied with.

(3) This section applies whether the trust of land and the trust of proceeds of sale are created, or arise, before or after the commencement of this Act.'

(8) In section 27—

  (a) for subsection (1) substitute—

      '(1) A purchaser of a legal estate from trustees of land shall not be concerned with the trusts affecting the land, the net income of the land or the proceeds of sale of the land whether or not those trusts are declared by the same instrument as that by which the trust of land is created.', and

(b) in subsection (2)—
- (i) for the words 'trust for sale' substitute 'trust',
- (ii) for the words 'the settlement of the net proceeds' substitute 'any trust affecting the net proceeds of sale of the land if it is sold', and
- (iii) for the words 'trustees for sale' substitute 'trustees'.

(9) In section 33—

- (a) for the words 'trustees for sale' substitute 'trustees of land', and
- (b) for the words 'on trust for sale' substitute 'land in trust'.

(10) In section 39(4), for the words 'trusts for sale' substitute 'trusts'.

(11) In section 42—

- (a) in subsection (1)(a), for the words 'trust for sale' substitute 'trust of land' and
- (b) in subsection (2)—
  - (i) in paragraph (a), for the words 'a conveyance on trust for sale' substitute 'land', and
  - (ii) in paragraph (b), for the words 'on trust for sale' substitute 'in trust'.

(12) In section 66(2), for the words 'trustee for sale' substitute 'trustee of land'.

(13) In section 102(1)—

- (a) for the words 'share in the proceeds of sale of the land and in the rents and profits thereof until sale' substitute 'interest under the trust to which the land is subject', and
- (b) for the words 'trustees for sale' substitute 'trustees'.

(14) In section 131, after the words 'but for this section' insert '(and paragraph 5 of Schedule 1 to the Trusts of Land and Appointment of Trustees Act 1996)'.

(15) In section 137—

- (a) in subsection (2)(ii), for the words 'the proceeds of sale of land' onwards substitute 'land subject to a trust of land, or the proceeds of the sale of such land, the persons to be served with notice shall be the trustees.', and
- (b) in subsection (5), for the words 'held on trust for sale' substitute 'subject to a trust of land'.

(16) In section 153(6)(ii), for the words 'in trust for sale' substitute 'as a trustee of land'.

The Land Registration Act 1925 (c 21)

5 (1) The Land Registration Act 1925 is amended as follows.

(2) In section 3(xv)(a)—

- (a) for the words 'held on trust for sale' substitute 'subject to a trust of land', and
- (b) for the words 'trustees for sale' substitute 'trustees'.

(3) In section 4, for the words 'trustee for sale' substitute 'trustee of land'.

(4) In section 8(1), for the words 'trustee for sale' substitute 'trustee of land'.

(5) In section 49—

(a)   in subsection (1)(d)—
    (i)   for the words 'the proceeds of sale of land held on trust for sale' substitute 'land subject to a trust of land', and
    (ii)   for the words 'disposition on trust for sale or of the' substitute 'trust or',
(b)   in subsection (2), for the words 'trust for sale' substitute 'trust of land',
(c)   in the proviso to that subsection, for the words 'a disposition on trust for sale or' substitute 'land, or trustees of', and
(d)   in subsection (3), for the words 'on trust for sale' substitute 'subject to a trust of land'.

(6) In section 78(4), at the end insert 'registered at the commencment of this Act'.

(7) In section 83, in paragraph (b) of the proviso to subsection (11), for the words 'held on trust for sale' substitute 'subject to a trust of land'.

(8) In section 94—

(a)   for subsection (1) substitute—
    '(1) Where registered and is subject to a trust of land, the land shall be registered in the names of the trustees.',
(b)   in subsection (3), for the words 'trust for sale, the trustees for sale' substitute 'trust of land, the trustees',
(c)   after that subsection insert—
    '(4) There shall also be entered on the register such restrictions as may be prescribed, or may be expedient, for the protection of the rights of the persons beneficially interested in the land.

    (5) Where a deed has been executed under section 16(4) of the Trusts of Land and Appointment of Trustees Act 1996 by trustees of land the registrar is entitled to assume that, as from the date of the deed, the land to which the deed relates is not subject to the trust unless he has actual notice that the trustees were mistaken in their belief that the land was conveyed to beneficiaries absolutely entitled to the land under the trust and of full age and capacity.', and
(d)   in accordance with the amendments made by paragraphs (a) to (c), in the sidenote, for the words 'on trust for sale' substitute 'in trust'.

(9) In section 95, for the words 'on trust for sale' substitute 'subject to a trust of land'.

(10) In paragraph (b) of the proviso to section 103(1)—

(a)   for the words 'on trust for sale' substitute 'subject to a trust of land', and
(b)   for the words 'the execution of the trust for sale' substitute 'a sale of the land by the trustees'.

(11) In section 111(1), for the words 'trustees for sale' substitute 'trustees of land'.

The Administration of Estates Act 1925 (c 25)

6   (1) The Administration of Estates Act 1925 is amended as follows.

(2) In section 39(1)—

(a)   in paragraph (i), at the beginning insert 'as respects the personal estate,',

(b)   for paragraph (ii) substitute—

'(ii)   as respects the real estate, all the functions conferred on them by Part I of the Trusts of Land and Appointment of Trustees Act 1996;', and

(c)   in paragraph (iii), for the words 'conferred by statute on trustees for sale, and' substitute 'necessary'.

(3) In section 41(6), for the words 'trusts for sale' substitute 'trusts'.

(4) In section 51(3)—

(a)   after the word 'married' insert 'and without issue',

(b)   before the word 'settlement', in both places, insert 'trust or', and

(c)   for the words 'an entailed interest' substitute 'a life interest'.

(5) In section 55(1), after paragraph (vi) insert—

'(via) 'Land' has the same meaning as in the Law of Property Act 1925;'.

The Green Belt (London and Home Counties) Act 1938 (c xciii)

7 In section 19(1) of the Green Belt (London and Home Counties) Act 1938—

(a)   for the words 'trustee for sale within the meaning of the Law of Property Act 1925' substitute 'trustee of land', and

(b)   for the words 'of a trustee for sale' substitute 'of a trustee of land'.

The Settled Land and Trustee Acts (Court's General Powers) Act 1943 (c 25)

8 In section 1 of the Settled Land and Trustee Acts (Court's General Powers) Act 1943—

(a)   in subsection (1)—

(i)   for the words 'trustees for sale of land' substitute 'trustees of land', and

(ii)   for the words 'land held on trust for sale' substitute 'land subject to a trust of land', and

(b)   in subsections (2) and (3), for the words 'trust for sale' substitute 'trust of land'.

The Historic Buildings and Ancient Monuments Act 1953 (c 49)

9 In sections 8(3), 8A(3) and 8B(3) of the Historic Buildings and Ancient Monuments Act 1953, for the words from 'held on' to 'thereof' substitute 'subject to a trust of land, are conferred by law on the trustees of land in relation to the land and to the proceeds of its sale'.

The Leasehold Reform Act 1967 (c 88)

10 In the Leasehold Reform Act 1967—

(a)   in section 6(1), for the words 'the statutory trusts arising by virtue of sections 34 to 36' substitute 'a trust arising under section 34 or section 36',

(b)   in section 24(1)(a), for the words 'held on trust for sale' substitute 'subject to a trust of land', and

(c)   in paragraph 7 of Schedule 2—

(i)   in sub-paragraph (1), for the words 'a disposition on trust for sale' substitute 'trust of land', and

(ii)   in sub-paragraph (3), for the words 'held on trust for sale' substitute 'subject to a trust of land'.

The Agriculture Act 1970 (c 40)

11 In section 33(2) of the Agriculture Act 1970—

(a)   for the words 'held under a trust for sale' substitute 'subject to a trust of land', and

(b)   for the words 'the trustees for sale' substitute 'the trustees of land'.

The Land Charges Act 1972 (c 61)

12 (1) The Land Charges Act 1972 is amended as follows.

(2) In section 2(4)(iii)(b), for the words 'trust for sale' substitute 'trust of land'.

(3) In section 6, after subsection (1) insert—

'(1A) No writ or order affecting an interest under a trust of land may be registered under subsection (1) above.'

The Land Compensation Act 1973 (c 26)

13 In subsection (2) of section 10 of the Land Compensation Act 1973, for the words 'held on trust for sale' substitute 'subject to a trust of land' and, in accordance with that amendement, in the sidenote of that section, for the words 'trusts for sale' substitute 'trusts of land'.

The Local Land Charges Act 1975 (c 76)

14 In section 11(2) of the Local Land Charges Act 1975, for the words 'held on trust for sale' substitute 'subject to a trust of land'.

The Rentcharges Act 1977 (c 30)

15 (1) The Rentcharges Act 1977 is amended as follows.

(2) In section 2(3), for paragraphs (a) and (b) substitute—

'(a)   in the case of which paragraph 3 of Schedule 1 to the Trusts of Land and Appointment of Trustees Act 1996 (trust in case of family charge) applies to the land on which the rent is charged;

(b)   in the case of which paragraph (a) above would have effect but for the fact that the land on which the rent is charged is settled land or subject to a trust of land;'.

(3) In section 10(2)(b), for the words 'trust for sale' substitute 'trust of land'.

The Interpretation Act 1978 (c 30)

16 In Schedule 1 to the Interpretation Act 1978, after the definition of 'The Treasury' insert—

' "Trust of Land" and "trustees of land", in relation to England and Wales, have the same meanings as in the Trusts of Land and Appointment of Trustees Act 1996.'

The Ancient Monuments and Archaeological Areas Act 1979 (c 46)

17 In the Ancient Monuments and Archaeological Areas Act 1979—

    (a)   in section 12(3), for the words 'trust for sale' substitute 'trust of land' and

    (b)   in section 18(4), for paragraph (b) substitute—

        '(b)   as trustees of land;'.

The Limitation Act 1980 (c 58)

18 In paragraph 9 of Schedule 1 to the Limitation Act 1980, for the words 'held on trust for sale' substitute 'subject to a trust of land'.

The Highways Act 1980 (c 66)

19 In section 87(4)(b) of the Highways Act 1980, for the words from 'and section 28' to 'apply' substitute 'applies'.

The Wildlife and Countryside Act 1981 (c 69)

20 In section 30(4)(c) of the Wildlife and Countryside Act 1981, for the words 'trusts for sale' substitute 'trusts of land'.

The Health and Social Services and Social Security Adjudications Act 1983 (c 41)

21 In section 22 of the Health and Social Services and Social Security Adjudications Act 1983

    (a)   in subsection (5)—

        (i)   for the words 'a joint tenant in the proceeds of sale of land held upon trust for sale' substitute 'an equitable joint tenant in land', and

        (ii)   for the words 'those proceeds' substitute 'the land',

    (b)   in subsection (6)—

        (i)   for the words 'a joint tenant in the proceeds of sale of land held upon trust for sale' substitute 'an equitable joint tenant in land',

        (ii)   for the words 'proceeds is' substitute 'land is', and

        (iii)   for the words 'interests in the proceeds' substitute 'interests in the land', and

    (c)   in subsection (8), for the words 'an interest in the proceeds of sale of land' substitute 'the interest of an equitable joint tenant in land'.

The Telecommunications Act 1984 (c 12)

22 In paragraph 4(10) of Schedule 2 to the Telecommunications Act 1984, for the words 'trusts for sale' substitute 'trusts of land'.

The Insolvency Act 1986 (c 45)

23 At the beginning of Chapter V of Part IX of the Insolvency Act 1986 insert—

'Rights under trusts of land

335A Rights under trusts of land

(1) Any application by a trustee of a bankrupt's estate under section 14 of the Trusts of Land and Appointment of Trustees Act 1996 (powers of court in relation to trusts

of land) for an order under that section for the sale of land shall be made to the court having jurisdiction in relation to the bankruptcy.

(2) On such an application the court shall make such order as it thinks just and reasonable having regard to—

- (a)   the interests of the bankrupt's creditors;
- (b)   where the application is made in respect of land which includes a dwelling house which is or has been the home of the bankrupt or the bankrupt's spouse or former spouse—
  - (i)   the conduct of the spouse or former spouse, so far as contributing to the bankruptcy,
  - (ii)   the needs and financial resources of the spouse or former spouse, and
  - (iii) the needs of any children; and
- (c)   all the circumstances of the case other than the needs of the bankrupt.

(3) Where such an application is made after the end of the period of one year beginning with the first vesting under Chapter IV of this Part of the bankrupt's estate in a trustee, the court shall assume, unless the circumstances of the case are exceptional, that the interests of the bankrupt's creditors outweigh all other considerations.

(4) The powers conferred on the court by this section are exercisable on an application whether it is made before or after the commencement of this section.'

The Patronage (Benifices) Measure 1986 (No. 3)

24   In section 33 of the Patronage (Benifices) Measure 1986—

- (a)   in subsection (1), for the words from 'held by any trustee' to 'capable of sale' substitute 'subject to a trust of land', and
- (b)   in subsection (2), for the words 'section 26(1) and (2) of the Law of Property Act 1925 (consents to the execution of a trust for sale)' substitute 'section 10 of the Trusts of Land and Appointment of Trustees Act 1996 (consents)'.

The Family Law Reform Act 1987 (c 42)

25   In section 19(2) of the Family Law Reform Act 1987, for the words 'which is used to create' substitute 'purporting to create'.

The Charities Act 1993 (c 10)

26   In section 23 of the Charities Act 1993—

- (a)   in subsection (1)(b), for the words 'trust for sale' substitute 'trust',
- (b)   in subsection (5), for the words 'trustee for sale' substitute 'trustee',
- (c)   in subsection (7), for the words 'trustees for sale' substitute 'trustees', and
- (d)   in subsection (9), for the words 'trust for sale' substitute 'trust'.

The Leasehold Reform, Housing and Urban Development Act 1993 (c 28)

27   (1) The Leasehold Reform, Housing and Urban Development Act 1993 is amended as follows.

(2) In Schedule 2—

(a) in paragraph 5(1) and (2), for the words 'held on trust for sale' substitute 'subject to a trust of land' (and, accordingly, in the heading immediately preceding paragraph 5 for the words 'on trust for sale' substitute 'in trust'),

(b) in paragraph 6, for the words 'as mentioned in paragraph 5(2)(b) above' substitute 'by the landlord on the termination of a new lease granted under Chapter II or section 93(4) (whether the payment is made in pursuance of an order under section 61 or in pursuance of an agreement made in conformity with paragraph 5 of Schedule 14 without an application having been made under that section)', and

(c) in paragraphs 7(2)(b) and 8(3)(b) and (4)(c), for '5(2)(b)' substitute '6'.

(3) In Schedule 14—

(a) in paragraph 7(1), for the words 'disposition on trust for sale' substitute 'trust of land', and

(b) in paragraph 9(1), for the words, 'held on trust for sale' substitute 'subject to a trust of land'.

SCHEDULE 4
Repeals

Section 25(2)

Chapter	Short title	Extent of repeal
3 & 4 Will 4 c 74.	The Fines and Recoveries Act 1833.	In section 1, the words ', and any undivided share thereof', in both places.
7 Will 4 & 1 Vict c 26.	The Wills Act 1837.	In section 1, the words 'and to any undivided share thereof,'. Section 32.
53 & 54 Vict c 39.	The Partnership Act 1890.	Section 22.
12 & 13 Geo 5 c 16.	The Law of Property Act 1922.	In section 188— in subsection (1), the words 'but not an undivided share in land;' and the words 'but not an undivided share thereof', and subsection (30).
15 & 16 Geo 5 c 18.	The Settled Land Act 1925.	Section 27. Section 29.
15 & 16 Geo 5 c 19.	The Trustee Act 1925.	In section 10(2)— in the first paragraph, the words 'by trustees or' and the words 'the trustees, or', and

Chapter	Short title	Extent of repeal
		in the second paragraph, the words from the beginning to 'mortgage; and'. In section 19(1), the words 'building or', in the second place. In section 68— in subsection (6), the words ', but not an undivided share in land' and the words ', but not an undivided share thereof', and in subsection (19), the word 'binding', the words ', and with or without power at discretion to postpone the sale' and the definition of 'trustees for sale'.
15 & 16 Geo 5 c 20.	The Law of Property Act 1925.	In section 3— subsections (1)(b) and (2), and in subsection (5), the words 'trustees for sale or other' In section 7(3), the second paragraph. In section 18— in subsection (1), the words from ', and personal estate' to 'payable', in the second place, and the words 'or is capable of being', and in subsection (2), the words 'of the settlement or the trustees for sale', in both places. Section 19. Section 23 (and the heading immediately preceding it).

Chapter	Short title	Extent of repeal
		Sections 25 and 26.
		Sections 28 to 30.
		Section 31(3).
		Section 32.
		In section 34—
		in subsection (3), the words from 'the trustees (if any)' to 'then to' and the words 'in each case', and subsection (4).
		Section 35.
		Section 42(6).
		In section 60, paragraphs (b) and (c) of the proviso to subsection (4).
		In section 130, subsections (1) to (3) and (6) (and the words 'Creation of' in the sidenote).
		Section 201(3).
		In section 205(1)—
		in paragraph (ix), the words 'but not an undivided share in land;' and the words 'but not an undivided share thereof',
		in paragraph (x), the words 'or in the proceeds of sale thereof', and
		in paragraph (xxix), the word 'binding', the words ', and with or without a power at discretion to postpone the sale' and the words 'and "power"' onwards.
15 & 16 Geo 5 c 21.	The Land Registration Act 1925.	In section 3—
		in paragraph (viii), the words 'but not an undivided share in land;',
		in paragraph (xi), the words 'or in the proceeds of sale thereof',

Chapter	Short title	Extent of repeal
		in paragraph (xiv), the words ', but not an undivided share thereof', and paragraphs (xxviii) and (xxix).
15 & 16 Geo 5 c 23.	The Administration of Estates Act 1925.	In section 3(1)(ii), the words 'money to arise under a trust for sale of land, nor'. In section 39(1)(i), the words from ', and such power' to 'legal mortgage'. In section 51— in subsection (3), the word 'settled', and subsection (4). In section 55(1)— in paragraph (vii), the words 'or in the proceeds of sale thereof', in paragraph (xiv), the word ' "land"', and paragraph (xxvii).
15 & 16 Geo 5 c 24.	The Universities and College Estates Act 1925.	In section 43(iv), the words ', but not an undivided share in land'.
16 & 17 Geo 5 c 11.	The Law of Property (Amendment) Act 1926.	In the Schedule, the entries relating to section 3 of the Settled Land Act 1925 and sections 26, 28 and 35 of the Law of Property Act 1925.
17 & 18 Geo 5 c 36.	The Landlord and Tenant Act 1927.	In section 13— in subsection (1), the words from '(either' to 'Property Act, 1925)', in subsection (2), the words ', trustee for sale, or personal representative', and in subsection (3), the words ', and "settled land"' onwards.

Chapter	Short title	Extent of repeal
22 & 23 Geo 5 c 27.	The Law of Property (Entailed Interests) Act 1932.	Section 1.
2 & 3 Geo 6 c 72.	The Landlord and Tenant (War Damage) Act 1939.	Section 3(c).
9 & 10 Geo 6 c 73.	The Hill Farming Act 1946.	Section 11(2).
12 & 13 Geo 6 c 74.	The Coast Protection Act 1949.	In section 11(2)(a)— the words ', by that section as applied by section twenty-eight of the Law of Property Act, 1925, in relation to trusts for sale,', and the words ', by that section as applied as aforesaid,'.
2 & 3 Eliz 2 c 56.	The Landlord and Tenant Act 1954.	In the Second Schedule, in paragraph 6— the words ', by that section as applied by section twenty-eight of the Law of Property Act, 1925, in relation to trusts for sale,', and the words ', by that section as applied as aforesaid,'.
7 & 8 Eliz 2 c 72.	The Mental Health Act 1959.	In Schedule 7, in Part I, the entries relating to sections 26 and 28 of the Law of Property Act 1925.
1964 No 2.	The Incumbents and Churchwardens (Trusts) Measure 1964.	In section 1, in the definition of 'land', the words 'nor an undivided share in land'.
1967 c 10.	The Forestry Act 1967.	In Schedule 2, paragraph 1(4).
1967 c 88.	The Leasehold Reform Act 1967.	In section 6(5)— the words ', or by that section as applied by section 28 of the Law of Property Act 1925 in relation to trusts for sale,',

Chapter	Short title	Extent of repeal
		the words 'or by that section as applied as aforesaid', and the words 'or by trustees for sale'. In Schedule 2, in paragraph 9(1)— the words ', or by that section as applied by section 28 of the Law of Property Act 1925 in relation to trusts for sale, and the words 'or by that section as applied as aforesaid'.
1969 c 10.	The Mines and Quarries (Tips) Act 1969.	In section 32(2)(a) and (b), the words ', by that section as applied by section 28 of the Law of Property Act 1925 in relation to trusts for sale'.
1970 c 40.	The Agriculture Act 1970.	In section 30— in subsection (1), the words '(including those provisions as extended to trusts for sale by section 28 of the Law of Property Act 1925)', and in subsection (2), the words 'the words from "(including those provisions" of "Law of Property Act 1925)" and'.
1972 c 61.	The Land Charges Act 1972.	In section 17(1), the definition of 'trust for sale'.
1976 c 31.	The Legitimacy Act 1976.	Section 10(4).
1976 c 36.	The Adoption Act 1976.	Section 46(5).
1977 c 42.	The Rent Act 1977.	In Schedule 2, in Part I, in paragraph 2(b), the words 'or, if it is held on trust for sale, the proceeds of its sale are'.

Chapter	Short title	Extent of repeal
1980 c 58.	The Limitation Act 1980.	In section 18— in subsection (1), the words ', including interests in the proceeds of the sale of land held upon trust for sale,', and in subsections (3) and (4), the words '(including a trust for sale)' and the words 'or in the proceeds of sale'. In section 38(1)— in the definition of 'land', the words ', including an interest in the proceeds of the sale of land held upon trust for sale,', and the definition of 'trust for sale'. In Schedule 1, in Part I, in paragraph 9— the words 'or in the proceeds of sale', the words 'or the proceeds', and the words 'or the proceeds of sale'.
1981 c 54.	The Supreme Court Act 1981.	In section 128, in the definition of 'real estate', in paragraph (b), the words 'money to arise under a trust for sale of land, nor'.
1983 c 41.	The Health and Social Services and Social Security Adjudications Act 1983.	Section 22(3).
1984 c 28.	The County Courts Act 1984.	In Schedule 2, in Part II, in paragraph 2— in sub-paragraph (1), the entry relating to section 30 of the Law of Property Act 1925, sub-paragraph (2), and

Chapter	Short title	Extent of repeal
		in sub-paragraph (3), '30(2)'.
1984 c 51.	The Inheritance Tax Act 1984.	In section 237(3), the words 'and undivided shares in land held on trust for sale, whether statutory or not,'.
1986 c 5.	The Agricultural Holdings Act 1986.	In section 89(1), the words 'or the Law of Property Act 1925'.
1986 c 45.	The Insolvency Act 1986.	In section 336— subsection (3), and in subsection (4), the words 'or (3)' and the words 'or section 30 of the Act of 1925'.
1988 c 50.	The Housing Act 1988.	In Schedule 1, in Part III, in paragraph 18(1)(b), the words 'or, if it is held on trust for sale, the proceeds of its sale are'.
1989 c 34.	The Law of Property (Miscellaneous Provisions) Act 1989.	In sections 1(6) and 2(6), the words 'or in or over the proceeds of sale of land'.
1990 c 8.	The Town and Country Planning Act 1990	In section 328— in subsection (1)(a), the words 'and by that section as applied by section 28 of the Law of Property Act 1928 in relation to trusts for sale', and in subsection (2)(a), the words 'and by that section as so applied'.
1991 c 31.	The Finance Act 1991.	Section 110(5)(b).
1993 c 10.	The Charities Act 1993.	Section 37(6). Section 39(5).
1993 c 28.	The Leasehold Reform, Housing and Urban Development Act 1993.	In section 93A(4)— the words ', or by that section as applied by section 28 of the Law

Chapter	Short title	Extent of repeal
		of Property Act 1925 in relation to trusts for sale', the words ', or by that section as so applied,', and the words 'or by trustees for sale'. In Schedule 2, paragraph 5(2)(b) and the word 'and' immediately preceding it.
1994 c 36.	The Law of Property (Miscellaneous Provisions) Act 1994.	In section 16— subsection (2), and in subsection (3), the words '; and subsection (2)' onwards.
1995 c 8.	The Agricultural Tenancies Act 1995.	In section 33— In subsections (1) and (2), the words from '(either' to 'Property Act 1925)', and in subsection (4), the definition of 'settled land' and the word 'and' immediately preceding it.
1996 c 53.	The Housing Grants, Construction and Regeneration Act 1996.	Section 55(4)(b). Section 73(3)(b). In section 98(2)(a), the words 'or to the proceeds of sale of the dwelling'.

Appendix II

Parliamentary Stages of the Trusts of Land and Appointment of Trustees Act

Lords	Date	Column	Volume
1st Reading	23.11.95	417	567 no 1647
2nd Reading	1.3.96	1717–1727	569 no 1657
Committee	25.3.96	1532–1559	570 no 1661
Report	22.4.96	954–971	571 no 1664
3rd Reading	7.5.96	94–102	572 no 1666
Commons Amendments	22.7.96	1174–1175	574 no 1676
Royal Assent	24.7.96	1496–1497	574 no 1676

Commons	Date	Column	Volume
1st Reading	7.5.96	*	
2nd Reading	18.6.96	787	279 no 1729
Committee	26.6.96	Standing Committee	NA
Report	16.7.96	1052	281 no 1733
3rd Reading	16.7.96	1052	281 no 1733

*The First Reading in the House of Commons was officially on 7 May 1996 but there is no recording of it in Hansard.

Appendix III

CHECKLISTS   Page
1 Existing trusts   135
2 New trusts   136

PRECEDENTS
1   Conveyance of land to beneficiaries absolutely entitled – section 6(2)   139
2   Conveyance upon partition – section 7(2)   141
3   Power of attorney delegating functions – section 9(1)   143
4   Statutory declaration – section 9(2)   145
5   Deed opting into consultation provisions – section 11(3)   146
6   Deed of discharge – section 16(4)   147
7   Directions by beneficiaries for appointment or retirement of trustees –
    section 19(2)   148
8   Directions where trustee mentally incapacitated – section 20(2)   149
9   Deed of retirement – section 19(3)   150
10   Withdrawal by beneficiary of direction – section 21(1)   152
11   Deed opting out of provision for appointment and retirement of
    trustees – section 21(6)   153
12   Clauses for incorporation in trust deeds   154

CHECKLISTS

1 CHECKLIST FOR EXISTING TRUSTS

Settlor's instructions	Action	Authority
1 Existing settlements If there is an alteration in a strict settlement or a derivative settlement, does the settlor wish to:		
(a) continue the settlement under the Settled Land Act; or	If so, the settlor need do nothing further.	s 2(3)
(b) opt for it to be a trust of land?	If so, the settlor must execute a deed to that effect: see Precedent 12.2.	s 2(3)
2 Consultation Does the settlor or do the surviving settlors wish to opt into the consultation provisions imposed on trustees in new trusts?	If so, the settlor(s) must execute a deed to that effect: see Precedent 5.	s 11(3)
3 Appointment and retirement of trustees Does the settlor or do the surviving settlors wish to opt out of the provisions relating to appointment and retirement of trustees?	If so, the settlor(s) must execute a deed to that effect: see Precedent 11.	s 21(6)–(8)

2 CHECKLIST FOR NEW TRUSTS

Settlor's instructions	Action	Authority
1 Duty to sell		
Does the settlor wish to impose an express trust for sale?	If so, he must insert in the trust deed a clause to that effect: see Precedent 12.1	
	If not, no action is required. There will be merely a power to sell and a power to retain: in the event of a dispute, there will be a stalemate unless there is an application to the court.	s 4(1)
2 Powers of trustees		
General powers: Does the settlor wish to restrict the wide powers given to the trustees?	If so, he must insert in the trust deed a clause specifying the restrictions on the trustees' powers: see, for example, Precedent 12.3.	s 8(1)
	If not, no action is required. The trustee will have the powers of an absolute owner.	s 6(1)
Partition: Does the settlor wish to restrict the power to partition the land?	If so, he must insert in the trust deed a clause specifying the nature of the restriction: see, for example, the restriction contained in Precedent 12.3.	s 8(1)
	If not, no action is required. The trustees will have power to partition the land, or part of it, provided that the beneficiaries are of full age and absolutely entitled in undivided shares to land subject to the trust, and consent.	s 7(1), (3)

Settlor's instructions	Action	Authority
Conveyance to the beneficiaries: Does the settlor wish to restrict the power of the trustees to force the beneficiaries to accept a conveyance of the land?	If so, he must insert in the trust a clause to that effect: see Precedent 12.3.	s 8(1)
	If not, no action is required. The trustees will have power to convey the land formerly subject to the trust to the beneficiaries without their request to do so or even their consent, provided that each is of full age, capacity and absolutely entitled to the land.	s 6(2)
Consent: Does the settlor wish to require the trustees to obtain the beneficiaries' consent before exercising any of their powers?	If so, he must insert in the trust deed a clause to that effect: see, for example, Precedent 12.3.	s 8(2)
	If not, no action is required. The trustees may exercise their powers without consent.	s 6

3 Rights of beneficiaries

Consultation: Does the settlor wish to exclude the need for the trustees to consult the beneficiaries?	If so, he must inset in the trust deed a clause specifically excluding that requirement: see, for example, Precedent 12.4.	s 11(2)
	If not, no action is required. The trustees must, so far as possible, consult the beneficiaries provided that they are of full age and beneficially entitled to an interest in possession of the land.	s 11(1)(a)
	The trustee must give effect to the beneficiaries' (or their majority's) wishes in so far as they are	s 11(1)(b)

Settlor's instructions	Action	Authority
	consistent with the general interest of the trust.	
Occupation by beneficiaries: Does the settlor wish to prevent the trustees from making the trust property available for occupation by a particular beneficiary?	If so, he must insert in the trust deed a clause to that effect: see, for example, Precedent 12.5.	s 13(1), (6)
	If not, no further action is required. A beneficiary who is beneficially entitled to an interest in possession of trust land may occupy the land provided that: – the purposes of the trust include making the land available for his occupation; or – the land is held by the trustees so as to be so available.	s 12(1)
Appointment of trustees: Does the settlor wish to exclude the right of beneficiaries to direct that a trustee be appointed or retire?	If so, he must insert in the trust deed a clause to that effect: see, for example, Precedent 12.6.	s 21(5)
	If not, no further action is required. The beneficiaries may give a written direction to the trustee or trustees: – to retire from the trust; and/or – to appoint by writing to be trustee(s) specified person(s).	s 19(2)
Duty to delegate: Does the settlor wish to impose a duty on trustees to delegate their powers to the life tenant?	If so, he must insert a clause to that effect: see, for example, Precedent 12.7.	s 9(1)
	If not, there will be a power to delegate.	

PRECEDENTS

1. CONVEYANCE OF LAND TO BENEFICIARIES ABSOLUTELY ENTITLED section 6(2)

THIS CONVEYANCE is made this   day of   199– **BETWEEN** (1) [*Name*] of [*Address*], [*Name*] of [*Address*] and [*Name*] of [*Address*] ('the Trustees') and (2) [*Name*] of [*Address*] and [*Name*] of [*Address*] ('the Beneficiaries')[1]

WHEREAS

(1) By the combined effect of the document[s] specified in the First Schedule hereto and of the Trusts of Land and Appointment of Trustees Act 1996 ('the 1996 Act') the Trustees are seised in fee simple of the land described in the Second Schedule hereto ('the Property') as trustees of a trust of land as defined by the 1996 Act ('the Trust')[2]

(2) The Beneficiaries [are of full age and capacity and] are absolutely entitled to the Property under the Trust and the Trustees have decided to convey the Property to them.[3]

NOW THIS DEED WITNESSETH as follows:

1 The Trustees pursuant to section 16(4) of the 1996 Act **HEREBY DECLARE** that they are discharged from the Trust in relation to the Property.[4]

2 In consideration of the premises the Trustees pursuant to section 6(2) of the 1996 Act **HEREBY CONVEY** the Property to the Beneficiaries with [limited/no] title guarantee To Hold unto the Beneficiaries in fee simple.[5]

[*3 Certificate for stamp duty.*]

IN WITNESS etc

FIRST SCHEDULE

[*List the document(s) constituting the Trust and the title of the Trustees*]

SECOND SCHEDULE

[*Description of the Property*]

1. Where there is more than one beneficiary, there will necessarily be a continuing trust (under Law of Property Act 1925, s 36(1), as amended), so that it will normally be more convenient simply to appoint the beneficiaries as new trustees, rather than conveying to them. This precedent will be useful where (a) there are plural beneficiaries, but they do not consent, or (b) there is a single beneficiary, so that the trust will be brought to an end.

2. This precedent should be strictly confined to cases where the 1996 Act has imposed a trust of land.

3. There is no need to recite the events whereby the beneficiaries have become absolutely entitled: clause 1 puts the trust behind the curtain for any future purchaser (see s 16(5) and Law of Property Act 1925, s 27(1), as amended). The words in square brackets are usually assumed by conveyancers (see Law of Property Act 1925, s 15), but their use in the Act (ss 6(2), 16(4), (5)), encourages their express use here.

4. A deed of discharge is required by s 16(4). A precedent of a separate deed is provided (Precedent 6), but it is not required to be a separate document, and there is no reason not to include it in this conveyance.

5. If there is only a single beneficiary, it will be appropriate to add 'freed and discharged from the Trust'.

2. CONVEYANCE UPON PARTITION   section 7(2)

THIS CONVEYANCE is made this   day of   199–
BETWEEN (1) [*Name*] of [*Address*], [*Name*] of [*Address*] and [*Name*] of
[*Address*] ('the Trustees') (2) [*Name*] whose registered office is at
[*Address*] ('the Mortgagee') and (3) [*Name*] of [*Address*] ('the
Beneficiary')[1]

WHEREAS

(1)   By the combined effect of the document[s] specified in the First
Schedule hereto and of the Trusts of Land and Appointment of Trustees
Act 1996 ('the 1996 Act') the Trustees are seised in fee simple of the land
described in the Second Schedule hereto ('the Property') with other land
as trustees of a trust of land as defined by the 1996 Act ('the Trust')[2]

(2)   The Trustees have with the consent[3] of all the beneficiaries under
the Trust partitioned the land subject to the Trust and the Beneficiary has
thereby become entitled to the Property absolutely subject to the payment
of £[   ] by way of equality money

(3)   By a Legal Charge dated   199– and made between
(1) the Trustees and (2) the Mortgagee ('the Mortgage') the Trustees
charged the property with repayment to the Mortgagee of the said sum of
£[   ] advanced to the Trustees by the Mortgagee

NOW THIS DEED WITNESSETH as follows:

1   The Trustees pursuant to section 16(4) of the 1996 Act **HEREBY
DECLARE** that they are discharged from the Trust in relation to the
Property.[4]

2   In consideration of the premises the Trustees pursuant to section 7(2)
of the 1996 Act **HEREBY CONVEY** the Property to the Beneficiary with
[limited/no] title guarantee To Hold unto the Beneficiary in fee simple
subject to the Mortgage but freed and discharged from the Trust.

3(a)   The Beneficiary **HEREBY COVENANTS** with the Mortgagee to
observe and perform all the obligations of the Mortgagor under the
Mortgage.

(b)   In consideration of the foregoing covenant the Mortgage **HEREBY
RELEASES** the Trustees and each of them from all their obligations
under the Mortgage.

[*4   Certificate for stamp duty.*]

IN WITNESS etc

FIRST SCHEDULE

[List the document(s) constituting the Trust and the title of the Trustees]

SECOND SCHEDULE

[Description of the Property]

---

1. The trustees have raised equality money by legal charge, and convey to a single beneficiary subject to the mortgage. The mortgagee joins in to release the trustees.
2. This precedent should be strictly confined to cases where the 1996 Act has imposed a trust of land.
3. See s 7(3).
4. A deed of discharge is required by s 16(4). A precedent of a separate deed is provided (Precedent 6), but it is not required to be a separate document, and there is no reason not to include it in this conveyance.

3. POWER OF ATTORNEY DELEGATING FUNCTIONS
section 9(1)

THIS POWER OF ATTORNEY is made this   day of   199–
BY [*Name*] of [*Address*], [*Name*] of [*Address*] and [*Name*] of [*Address*] ('the Trustees')[1]

WHEREAS

(1) The Trustees are the trustees of the trust of land ('The Trust')[2] created by a Conveyance dated the   199– and made between (1) [*Name*] and (2) the Trustees

(2) [*Name*] of [*Address*] and [*Name*] of [*Address*] ('the Beneficiaries')[3] are beneficiaries of full age and capacity entitled to interests in possession in land subject to the Trust

NOW THIS DEED WITNESSETH as follows:

1 The Trustees pursuant to section 9(1) of the Trusts of Land and Appointment of Trustees Act 1996 **HEREBY APPOINT** the Beneficiaries jointly [and severally][4] to be their attorneys for the purpose of performing in the name and on behalf of the Trustees:

> all their functions as trustees of the Trust relating to the land subject to the Trust except that of receiving and giving a receipt for capital monies[5]

> [*or*] the following functions of the Trustees relating to the land subject to the Trust: [*specify particular functions, eg*]
> (a) power to sell the land at the best price obtainable;
> (b) power to let the land for the best rent obtainable without taking a fine for any term not exceeding 25 years;
> (c) power to partition the land pursuant to section 7 of the said Act; [etc].

[2 This Power shall automatically determine:

> (a) at the expiration of 10 years from the date hereof,[6] or
> (b) if it is revoked in relation to either of the Beneficiaries.[7]]

IN WITNESS etc

1. All the trustees must give the power jointly (s 9(3)).
2. This precedent should be strictly confined to cases where the 1996 Act has imposed a trust of land.
3. The beneficiaries must be entitled to an interest in possession in the land (s 9(1)). The Act does not forbid delegation to a single beneficiary, but in most cases at least two will be desirable.
4. Several, or joint and several, delegation is contemplated by s 9(4), but is unlikely to be advisable.
5. Despite the generality of the wording of s 9(1), it seems the intention behind the closing words of s 9(7) is to prevent delegation of the function of receiving capital monies (see Hansard, col 1536). Whether the words achieve that intention may be doubted, but it is safest to restrict the power in this way.
6. The power may be limited or indefinite in duration (s 9(5)).
7. Since the power is not expressed to be irrevocable, any of the trustees can revoke it (s 9(3)). For further circumstances involving revocation see s 9(3) and (4).

4. STATUTORY DECLARATION section 9(2)

I, [*Name*] of [*Address and Description*] **DO SOLEMNLY AND SINCERELY DECLARE** as follows:[1]

1 By a Conveyance [or as the case may be] dated the 199–, and made between (1) [*Name*], [*Name*] and [*Name*] (2) myself, I acquired the land comprised therein, which had immediately beforehand been subject to a trust of land. The said Conveyance was executed not by the trustees of the trust, but by [*Name*] and [*Name*],[2] to whom they had delegated certain of their functions relating to the land (including their powers to sell and convey it) by a Power of Attorney dated 199–, which was granted pursuant to section 9(1) of the Trusts of Land and Appointment of Trustees Act 1996.

2 At the time of that acquisition I dealt with the said [*Name*] and [*Name*] in good faith, and I had no knowledge that they were not persons to whom those functions could properly be delegated in that manner.

AND I MAKE etc[3]

---

1. This precedent is designed to exploit the conclusive presumption provided by s 9(2). It must be made by a third party who has dealt with beneficiaries acting under a power of attorney granted under s 9(1) (see Precedent 3). The presumption takes effect in favour of a subsequent purchaser, but it must be made by the third party who dealt with the beneficiary.
2. If the power of attorney does not delegate the power to receive capital moneys (see Precedent 3, footnote 5), there will have been no point in the attorneys conveying, since the trustees will have had to be parties in order to give the receipt. The occasions for this Precedent may, therefore, be very few.
3. The declaration can be made as late as three months after the completion of the subsequent purchase, but it will be prudent to make it at the time of the original dealing, since it can be made only by the third party himself (not his personal representatives).

5. DEED OPTING INTO CONSULTATION PROVISIONS
section 11(3)

THIS DEED is made this   day of   199–
BY [BETWEEN (1)] [*Name*] of [*Address*] ('the Settlor') [and (2) [*Name*]
of [*Address*], [*Name*] of [*Address*] and [*Name*] of [*Address*] ('the
Trustees')][(1)]

SUPPLEMENTAL to a Conveyance dated the   199–
and made between (1) the Settlor and [*Name*] and (2) the Trustees
whereby the Settlor and the said [*Name*] settled the land thereby
conveyed upon a trust of land ('the Trust') as defined by the Trusts of
Land and Appointment of Trustees Act 1996 ('the 1996 Act')[(2)]

WHEREAS:

(1) The said [*Name*] died on the   199–[(3)]
[(2) The Trustees are the trustees of the Trust]
(3) The Settlor wishes the Trustees to observe the obligations to consult
the beneficiaries imposed by section 11(1) of the 1996 Act.

NOW THIS DEED WITNESSETH and the Settlor **HEREBY** irrevocably[(4)]
DIRECTS AND DECLARES that section 11(1) of the 1996 Act shall
henceforth apply to the Trust.

IN WITNESS etc

---

1. It is assumed that the trust was created by a pre-1996 Act conveyance, made by two parents in favour of their children: one parent has since died. It is not essential for the trustees to be parties, but it is obviously convenient, and good practice.
2. This precedent should be strictly confined to cases where the 1996 Act has imposed a trust of land.
3. Section 11(3)(b) authorises the survivor of joint settlors to opt in.
4. This word serves as a reminder that s 11(3) prevents the reservation of a power of revocation.

6. DEED OF DISCHARGE   section 16(4)

THIS DEED OF DISCHARGE is made this   day of
              199– **BY** [*Name*] of [*Address*], [*Name*] of [*Address*] and
[*Name*] of [*Address*] ('the Trustees')[1]

WHEREAS by the combined effect of the document[s] specified in the
First Schedule hereto and of the Trusts of Land and Appointment of
Trustees Act 1996 ('the 1996 Act') the Trustees are seised in fee simple of
the land described in the Second Schedule hereto ('the Property') as
trustees of a trust of land as defined by the 1996 Act ('the Trust')[2]

NOW THIS DEED WITNESSETH and the Trustees pursuant to section
16(4) of the 1996 Act **HEREBY DECLARE** that they are discharged from
the Trust in relation to the Property.

IN WITNESS etc

FIRST SCHEDULE

[*List the document(s) constituting the Trust and the title of the Trustees*]

SECOND SCHEDULE

[*Description of the Property*]

---

1. This precedent complies with the trustees' obligation under s 16(4), which is part of the machinery for protecting purchasers when the land is conveyed to beneficiaries. In most cases, a separate deed will not be necessary, and a clause in the conveyance will suffice. (See Precedents 1 and 2.)
2. This precedent should be strictly confined to cases where the 1996 Act has imposed a trust of land.

7.   DIRECTIONS BY BENEFICIARIES FOR APPOINTMENT OR RETIREMENT OF TRUSTEES   section 19(2)

To: [*Name*] [*and/or*]
   [*The Trustees*]

We, the undersigned, being beneficiaries of full age and capacity [between us absolutely[1]] entitled to [an interest in] the property comprised in the trust [of land][2] ('the Trust') created by the document[s] specified in the Schedule hereto **HEREBY DIRECT** (pursuant to section 19(2) of the Trusts of Land and Appointment of Trustees Act 1996) that

> [*Name*] is to retire from the Trust[3]
> [*and/or*]
> the Trustees are to appoint by writing [*Name*] to be a trustee of the Trust[4]

SCHEDULE

[*List the document(s) constituting the Trust*]

Dated:

Signed:
     (1)
     (2)
     (3) etc

---

1. Directions must be given by beneficiaries who are between them absolutely entitled, but not necessarily by the same document. Similar documents may be signed by all or any one or more of the beneficiaries (s 21(1)), provided that they all give the same directions (s 21(2)).
2. Sections 19 and 20 apply generally to all trusts, unless they have been opted out, and not merely to trusts of land. These directions may therefore be given in relation to trusts of pure personalty.
3. This direction must be given to the trustee directed to retire (s 19(2)(a)).
4. This direction must be given to all the trustees for the time being, or to the personal representatives of the last surviving trustee (s 19(2)(b)).

8. DIRECTIONS WHERE TRUSTEE MENTALLY INCAPACITATED section 20(2)

To: [*Name*], the Receiver of [*Name*] [or
           the Attorney of [*Name*] under an Enduring Power of
           Attorney, or
           a person authorised for this purpose under Part VII of the
           Mental Health Act 1983]

WE,[1] the undersigned, being beneficiaries of full age and capacity
[between us absolutely] entitled to [an interest in] the property
comprised in the trust [of land] ('the Trust') created by the document[s]
specified in the Schedule hereto **HEREBY DIRECT** (pursuant to section
20(2) of the Trusts of Land and Appointment of Trustees Act 1996) that
you are to appoint [*Name*] by writing to be a trustee of the Trust in place
of [*Name*], who is incapable by reason of mental disorder of exercising his
functions as trustee of the Trust.

SCHEDULE

[*List the document(s) constituting the Trust*]

Dated:

Signed:
           (1)
           (2)
           (3) etc

---

1. The categories of person to whom the directions can be given are listed in s 20(2). Footnotes
   1 and 2 to the preceding Precedent apply equally here.

9. DEED OF RETIREMENT

section 19(3)

THIS DEED OF RETIREMENT is made this   day of   199–
BETWEEN (1) [*Name*] of [*Address*] ('the Retiring Trustee') (2) [*Name*] of
[*Address*] ('the Continuing Trustee') and (3) [*Name*] of [*Address*] ('the
New Trustee')[1]

SUPPLEMENTAL to a Trust Deed dated the   19— and
made between (1) [*Name*] and (2) [*Name*] and [*Name*] ('the Settlement')
[and to the deeds affecting the trusteeship of the Settlement specified in
the Schedule hereto]

WHEREAS

(1)   The Retiring Trustee and the Continuing Trustee are the trustees of
the Settlement.

(2)   There is no person nominated by the Settlement for the purpose of
appointing new trustees.

(3)   By written directions dated the   199– the
Beneficiaries under the Settlement (being of full age and capacity and
between them absolutely entitled to the property subject to the
Settlement):

    (a)   pursuant to section 19(2)(a) of the Trusts of Land and Appointment
         of Trustees Act 1996 ('the 1996 Act') directed the Retiring Trustee to
         retire from the trusts of the Settlement and
    (b)   pursuant to section 19(2)(b) of the 1996 Act directed the Trustees to
         appoint the New Trustee a trustee of the Settlement.

(4)   The Retiring Trustee is satisfied that reasonable arrangements have
been made for the protection of his rights in connection with the trusts of
the Settlement.[2]

NOW THIS DEED executed pursuant to section 19(3) of the 1996 Act
WITNESSETH as follows:

1   The Retiring Trustee and the Continuing Trustee **HEREBY APPOINT**
the New Trustee to be an additional trustee of the trusts of the
Settlement.[3]

2   The Retiring Trustee **HEREBY DECLARES** that he retires from the
said trusts.

3   The Continuing Trustee and the New Trustee **HEREBY CONSENT** to
the retirement of the Retiring Trustee.[4]

4   All parties mutually **COVENANT** to do all things necessary to vest in the Continuing Trustee and the New Trustee jointly all such property subject to the said trusts as does not impliedly vest by operation of this Deed.[5]

IN WITNESS etc.

SCHEDULE

[*List the document(s) (if any) effecting the devolution of the trusteeship*]

---

1. This is the compulsory deed required by s 19(3) from a trustee who has been removed. It is assumed that directions have been given under both s 19(2)(a) and (b).
2. Without such arrangements the retiring trustee is not bound to execute this deed (s 19(3)(b)). He will no doubt want indemnities and a release, which will be best placed in a separate document.
3. This sequence of operations seems best calculated to satisfy s 19(3)(c) and (d), although the opposite order of appointment and retirement would probably serve.
4. In view of the terms of s 19(3)(d), this clause may be strictly unnecessary, but it is included as a matter of caution in the interests of certainty and of the retiring trustee, since he will not be discharged if this section is not satisfied.
5. This clause is a reminder of the parties' obligations under s 19(4), and is strictly unnecessary. Most land will vest by implication under s 40(1)(b) of the Trustee Act 1925.

10. WITHDRAWAL BY BENEFICIARY OF DIRECTION
section 21(1)

To: [*Name*] [*and/or*]
   [*The Trustees*]

I,[1] the undersigned, being a beneficiary of full age and capacity entitled to an interest in the property comprised in the trust [of land] ('the Trust') created by the document(s) specified in the Schedule hereto **HEREBY WITHDRAW** the direction dated the   199– which I gave to you pursuant to section 19(2) of the Trusts of Land and Appointment of Trustees Act 1966 requiring

[*Name*] to retire from the Trust
[*and/or*]
the Trustees to appoint by writing [*Name*] to be a trustee of the Trust

SCHEDULE

[*List the document(s) constituting the Trust*]

Dated:

Signed:

---

1. Section 21(1) contemplates that a direction under s 19 or s 20 may be withdrawn in writing before it is acted on. This precedent is drafted only under s 19, but can be adapted to s 20. It should be given to the same persons as the original direction.

11. DEED OPTING OUT OF PROVISIONS FOR APPOINTMENT AND RETIREMENT OF TRUSTEES

section 21(6)

THIS DEED is made the   day of   199– **BY** [**BETWEEN** (1)] [*Name*] of [*Address*] ('the Settlor') [and (2) [*Name*] of [*Address*], [*Name*] of [*Address*] and [*Name*] of [*Address*] ('the Trustees')][1]

SUPPLEMENTAL to a Trust Deed dated the   199– and made between (1) the Settlor and (2) the Trustees whereby the Settlor settled the Trust Fund upon the trusts therein mentioned ('the Settlement')

WHEREAS:

[(1) The Trustees are the trustees of the Settlement]

(2) The Settlor does not wish sections 19 or 20 of the Trusts of Land and Appointment of Trustees Act 1996 ('the 1996 Act') to apply to the Settlement [except to the extent indicated below[2]]

NOW THIS DEED WITNESSETH and the Settlor **HEREBY** irrevocably[3] **DIRECTS AND DECLARES** that sections 19 and 20 of the 1996 Act shall not apply to the trusts of the Settlement [except to the following extent:

(a) the power in section 19(2)(a) to direct a trustee to retire shall apply but only in the case of [*Name*];

(b) if [*Name*] is directed to retire section 19(3) and (4) shall apply accordingly].

IN WITNESS etc

---

1. It is assumed that the trust was created by a pre-1996 Act conveyance, made by a single settlor. It is not essential for the trustees to be parties, but it is obviously convenient, and good practice.

2. Section 21(6) indicates that ss 19 and 20 can be disapplied in whole or in part. The partial retention of s 19(2)(a) is chosen for drafting purposes only.

3. This word serves as a reminder that s 21(7) prevents the reservation of a power of revocation.

12. CLAUSES FOR INCORPORATION IN TRUST DEEDS

12.1 Trust to Sell[(1)]
The Trustees shall hold the property upon trust to sell it.

12.2 Opting out of Settled Land Act 1925 (s 2(3))
Notwithstanding section 2(2) of the Trusts of Land and Appointment of Trustees Act 1996 this trust shall be a trust of land and not a settlement for the purposes of the Settled Land Act 1925 [and the Trustees shall hold the property upon trust to sell it].

12.3 Excluding/Restricting Statutory Powers and Requiring Consents (s 8(1), (2))[(2)]
(a) Sections [6(2) and 7(3)] of the Trusts of Land and Appointment of Trustees Act 1996 shall not apply to this trust and accordingly the Trustees [shall not convey any land to a beneficiary against his will but may partition land without the consent of any beneficiary].

(b) The Trustees shall not exercise the power [to purchase land by way of investment (conferred by section 6(3) and (4)(a) of the said Act) without the prior written consent of [Name]].

12.4 Excluding/Restricting Obligation to Consult Beneficiaries (s 11(2)(a))
Section 11(1) of the Trusts of Land and Appointment of Trustees Act 1996 shall not apply to this trust [except when the trustees are considering the exercise of their power to sell any dwellinghouse which is subject to the trust] and accordingly the Trustees may exercise all their [other] powers relating to land without consulting any beneficiary.

12.5 Excluding/Restricting Beneficiaries' Rights to Occupy Land (s 13(1), (6)) [(3)]
Notwithstanding section 12 of the Trusts of Land and Appointment of Trustees Act 1996 [Name] shall not be entitled to occupy any dwellinghouse which is at any time subject to this trust [nor shall any other beneficiary who does occupy any such dwellinghouse be required to compensate him or to forgo in his favour any benefit hereunder].

12.6 Excluding/Restricting Trustee Appointment Provisions (s 21(5))
Section [19(2)(a)] of the Trusts of Land and Appointment of Trustees Act 1996 shall not apply to this trust [except in the case of a trustee who is over the age of 70 and accordingly the beneficiaries may not direct any other trustee to retire].

12.7 Requiring Delegation under s 9(1)[4]

[So long as he is beneficially entitled in possession to his interest under this trust[5]] the Trustees shall delegate to [*Name*] all their functions relating to land except that of receiving and giving a receipt for capital monies.[6]

---

1. This clause will not prevent the trust from being a trust of land. Its object is to incorporate the time-honoured structure of trust to sell, with power to postpone (implied by s 3), which provides the basic presumption for resolving disagreements between the Trustees (see *Re Mayo* [1943] Ch 302). The Act provides no such structure for trusts of land, so that without a provision of this kind disagreement is likely to lead to paralysis.
2. It will surely be unusual to exclude ss 6 and 7 entirely, since the other principal statutory source of powers for trustees (LPA 1925, s 28) is repealed.
3. The Act gives this power to the Trustees, who must not exercise it unreasonably (s 13(2)). A clause of this kind, imposing the Settlor's wishes, seems permissible.
4. This clause is included in deference to the notion, aired in the House of Lords (see Hansard, cols 1535 and 1536), that the obsolete structure of a strict settlement could be reproduced by means of compulsory delegation to a beneficiary under s 9(1). Expert advice should be taken before attempting such a scheme. It is not achieved by this simple draft (eg functions relating to land will not include the tenant for life's important power under Settled Land Act 1925, s 75(2) to direct application of the proceeds).
5. This phrase deviates from Settled Land Act 1925, s 106 (prohibiting curtailment of the tenant for life's powers).
6. For the reasoning behind this exception, see Precedent 3 footnote 5.

INDEX

References are to paragraph numbers except where they are in *italics* which are references to page numbers.

Agent
  use of, by trustee   5.8.1, *see also*
    Delegation
Annuitant   5.8.2, 7.1, 7.5.1, 7.6.6

Bankrupt
  trustee is   4.3.1
  trustee of a, considerations for   2.2.10,
    6.6
    matters for court   6.6
Bare trust   1.3, 1.4.4
  overreaching, and   8.2.2
  trust of land, as   2.2.1, 3.1
Beneficiary
  best interests, duty of trustees   7.6.1
  consent of, general   7.6.3
  consultation with, *see* Consultation
  conveyance to   5.4, 5.6, 6.5.3
    consent to   2.2.6, 5.6
    duty to secure vesting in selves   5.4,
      7.8
    no consultation duty,
      circumstances   2.2.8, 2.2.10,
      5.7.5
    partition, after   2.2.6, 5.6, 8.3.3
  court, application to   6.2, 7.9
  definition   5.7.3, 5.8.2, 7.1
    beneficially entitled, distinction for
      5.8.2, 7.1
  delegation to, *see* Delegation
  directions for appointment/retirement of
    trustees   2.2.13, 4.4, 4.5, 7.7
    exclusion of power   4.1, 4.10.3,
      4.10.4, App III
    preconditions   4.1, 4.5, 4.7
    replacement of mentally disordered
      trustee, for   4.6
    retirement provisions   4.7
    rules   4.9
    separate directions   4.9, 4.10.1
    trust created before Act   4.1
    withdrawal of   4.9
  dispute between, matters for court
    7.9
  minor   2.2.6
  occupation by   2.2.9, 7.5

purchase of land for   5.5
  see also Occupation
rights   7.3
  exclusion of   7.10.1, App III
  previous law, under   7.2
  trustees to have regard to   5.7.3,
    7.6.2
  see also Consultation; Occupation
termination of trust by   4.3
wishes of
  court regard to   2.2.10, 6.5.2, 6.5.3
  trustees' regard to   7.5.1, 7.6.4
Bill   1.4.3, 1.4.5, 1.4.6, App II

Charging order
  not registrable   7.4
Charitable trusts
  land held on
    disposition of   3.3.4
    new law   2.2.2, 2.2.6, 3.3.4
    old law   3.3.4
    purchaser of   8.6
Charity Commissioners
  order of, restricts trustees   5.7.4
Chequers and Chevening estates   3.5
Commencement   2.1
Conditional fee simple   3.3.6
Consent
  beneficiaries', to conveyance to   2.2.6,
    5.6
  order obviating need to obtain
    2.2.10, 6.3
  purchaser not concerned   8.3.3
  trustees' act, to   2.2.7
Constructive trust   3.1, 3.2
Consultation
  beneficiaries, with, duty of trustees
    2.2.8, 5.1, 5.7.5, 7.6.4
    exceptions   2.2.8, 2.2.10, 5.7.5,
      5.10.1, 7.6.4
    existing trust, opting in   5.10.2
    purchaser not concerned   8.3.2
    transitional provisions   7.6.4
    when implied (new law)   7.6.4
  contracting-in provisions   2.2.8, 5.7.5,
    7.6.4
  deed, irrevocability of   7.6.4

Consultation *cont*
  exclusion of power in trust
     instrument   2.2.8, 5.1, 5.7.5
     advisability of   5.10.1
  order obviating need for   2.2.10, 6.3
Conversion, doctrine of   1.2.5, 7.4
  abolition   2.2.3, 7.4
     tax consequences   7.4
     transitional   2.2.12, 5.9, 7.4
Co-owners
  conveyance to
     beneficial ownership, and new law
        3.7.4
     duty to sell, inclusion in   3.8.3
  new law   3.2, 3.7.4
  old law   1.2.5
Court powers, *see* Powers of court
Creation
  trust of land, of   3.2
Creditor
  bankrupt, of   6.6
  secured, of beneficiary, right to apply to
     court   6.2
  court to have regard to interests
     6.5.1
Crown
  Act binds   2.1

Death
  tenant for life, of   1.2.3
  trustee, of   4.3.1, 4.4
  trusts of land arising on   5.9, *see also*
     Personal representative(s); Will
Delegation   2.2.6, 5.8, 7.6.6
  duties and liabilities of beneficiary-
     delegate   5.8.2
  exclusion of power   5.8.1
  liability of trustees   2.2.6, 5.8.1, 5.8.2
  power, existing law continuing   5.8.1
  power, to beneficiaries, new law   5.8.2,
     7.6.6
     'beneficiary'   5.8.2
  jointly or separately   5.8.2
  power of attorney, by   2.2.6, 5.8.1
     joint, by all trustees   5.8.2
     revocation of   2.2.6, 5.8.2
  previous law   5.8.2, 7.2
  principle   5.8.1
  sub-delegation etc not permitted
     5.8.2, 7.6.6
  third party, protection of   8.4
  transitional   5.8.2

Determinable fee simple   3.3.6
Discharge, deed of
  purchaser's reliance on   2.2.11, 8.1,
     8.5.1, 8.5.3
Dwelling-house
  bankrupt or spouse, of, court powers
     6.6

Ecclesiastical trusts
  land held on
     disposition of   3.3.4
     new law   2.2.2, 2.2.6, 3.3.4
     old law   3.3.4
     purchaser of   8.6
Entailed interest   3.3.5
Equitable duties
  trustees, of   5.7.2, 7.6.1
Equitable interests
  trust for sale, application where arise by
     way of trust   3.2

Family charge
  land subject to, old and new law   3.3.3

House ownership
  statistics   1.2.5

Incumbrance
  land subject to, trustees' discretion
     2.2.6, 5.6
Insolvency, *see* Bankrupt
Insurance
  trustees' power   5.2
Interest (land)
  entailed, grant no longer possible
     3.3.5
  equitable   3.2
  concurrent and successive   1.2.1,
     1.2.4, 3.2
Intestacy   3.7.2
Investment
  purchase of land for   2.2.6, 3.7.2, 5.5

Land
  see also Incumbrance; Occupation;
     Partition of land; Purchase of land;
     Registered land; Sale of land
  meaning for Land Charges Act   7.4

Law Commission
consultation requirement 7.6.4
court powers, comments on 6.1
lease, purchase by trustees, views on 5.5
occupation rents, on 7.5.1
recommendations 1.1, 1.2.3, 1.4.1
Report on overreaching 1.4.4, 7.5.2
Report on trusts of land 1.4.3
Leasehold
delegation of management powers 5.8.2
purchase by trustees 5.5
Lord Chancellor's Department
changes made by 1.4.5

Marriage
land charge in consideration of 3.3.3
Mental disorder
trustee, of 2.2.13, 4.3.1,.4.6
Minor 2.2.6, 2.2.7
consent, and 7.6.3, 8.3.3
conveyance to, alone or jointly 3.3.2, 4.3.3
legal estate cannot be held by 4.2
partition of land, and share vested in 5.6
trustee, cannot be 4.2, 4.3.1, 4.3.3
welfare of, court to have regard to 2.2.10, 6.5.1
Mortgage
redemption barred, trust of land imposed 3.7.1
trustees' position, existing law 5.2

Occupation
beneficiary is in, rights 2.2.9, 7.5.1
overriding interest, as 8.2.1
beneficiary's right 2.2.9, 7.5
compensation for exclusion 7.5.1
conditions, attachment of 2.2.9, 7.5.1
rent and other payments 2.2.9, 7.5.1
restriction or exclusion of 7.5.1
suitability of land, and 7,5,1
two or more entitled 2.2.9, 2.2.10, 7.5.1
purchase of land for 5.5
purchaser, protection of 7.5.2
wishes of beneficiary, court regard to 2.2.10, 6.5.2, 7.9

Order
court power to make 2.2.10, 6.1 et seq, *see also* Powers of court
trustees' powers subject to 5.7.4
Outgoings
payment by beneficiary 2.2.9, 7.5.1
Overreaching
consent to, trust stipulating need for 7.5.2
effect of 7.5.2
family charge 3.3.3
Law Commission Report 1.4.4
protection of purchaser, for 8.2
two trustees, need for 1.2.5
Overriding interest 8.2.1

Partition of land
consent to 7.6.3
purchaser not concerned with consents 8.3.3
trustees' power 2.2.6, 5.6
Personal property
trust of land mixed with 3.1
appointment of new trustees 4.1
beneficiary of personal property, right to apply to court 7.9
land purchased by trustees 3.7.2
trustees of trust of 4.2, 4.4
Personal representative(s) 5.9
appointment of trustee by 4.4–4.6
property to be held on trust by, on intestacy 3.7.3
provisions applying to 2.2.12, 5.9
powers of trustees 5.9
Power of appointment
exercise of, after Act 3.3.8
Power of attorney
beneficiary ceasing to be interested, effect 2.2.6
delegation by trustees by 2.2.6, 5.8, 5.10.3, *see also* Delegation
liabilities of trustee and beneficiary 2.2.6
precedent App III
purchaser, subsequent, and 2.2.6
revocation and lapse 2.2.6, 5.8.2
third party dealing with donee 2.2.6, 8.4
Power of attorney, enduring
trustee, for 2.2.13, 4.6
Powers of court 2.2.10, 6.1 et seq
application to court
determination of 6.5

Powers of court *cont*
  application to court *cont*
    matters to take into account   6.5.1–
      6.5.3, 7.9
    occupation of beneficiary, relating to,
      see Occupation
    rights of beneficiaries   6.5.2, 6.5.3
    trustee in bankruptcy, by   6.6
    who may make   6.2, 7.9
  exclusion of beneficiary in occupation, as
    to   7.5.1
  exercise of power of trustees, as to
    6.3
  existing provisions (continuing)   6.3
  original provision, uncertainties in
    6.1
  prevention or enforcement of sale,
    for   6.3
  re-enacted provision with
    amendments   6.2 et seq
  relief of obligation on trustee, as to
    6.3
  trustee's appointment or retirement, as
    to   6.4, 7.9
  vesting order, property to
    beneficiaries   6.1, 7.8
Powers of trustees   2.2.6, 3.6, 5.1 et seq
  absolute owner, of (new law)   5.2,
    5.7.2
  conflict of interests, and   5.7.2
  conveyance to beneficiaries   5.4
  delegation of, *see* Delegation
  exclusion of beneficiary from
    occupation   7.5.1, *see also*
    Occupation
  incumbrances, as to   2.2.6, 5.6
  insurance, for   5.2
  limitations on   5.2, 5.7
    consultation duty   2.2.8, 5.1, 5.7.5
    duty to bring to attention of
      purchaser   7.6.5
    enactments, orders and rules,
      restrictions in   5.7.4, 8.3.5
    equitable duties   5.7.2
    purchaser, and   7.6.5, 8.3.4, 8.3.5
    rights of beneficiaries, regard to
      5.7.3
    trust instrument, in   5.7.1, 8.3.4
  old law   5.2
  overriding duty   5.2, 5.7.2
  partition of land, for   2.2.6, 5.6, 8.3.3
    minor, share vested in   5.6
  purchase of land, for   2.2.6, 3.7.2, 5.5
    occupation of beneficiaries, for   5.5

  sale or retention of land   5.3
  unanimity and exercise of   5.7.2,
    5.10.4
Public trusts
  land held on
    disposition of   3.3.4
    new law   2.2.2, 2.2.6, 3.3.4
    old law   3.3.4
    purchaser of   8.6
Purchase of land
  trustees, by   2.2.6, 3.7.2, 5.5
    foreign country, in   5.5
Purchaser (of trust land)
  meaning   8.1
  protection of   2.2.6, 2.2.11, 4.1,
    8.1–8.7
    charitable etc trusts   8.6
    consent of, or consultation with,
      beneficiary, and   5.6, 8.1, 8.3
    deed of discharge, reliance on
      2.2.11, 8.1, 8.7.1
    beneficiary in occupation, where
      7.5.2
    delegation of trustees' powers, on
      8.4
    payment of trust money to two
      trustees   8.1, 8.2
    restrictions on trustees' powers,
      and   7.6.5, 8.1 8.3.4
    statutory declaration from third
      party   8.4, 8.7.2, App III
    termination of trust, and   8.5
    trust for sale/strict settlement   8.2.1
    trust of land   8.2.2, 8.7

Receiver
  trustee, for   2.2.13, 4.6
Reform
  see also Law Commission
  responses   1.4.2–1.4.6
  suggestions   1.4.1
Registered land
  beneficiaries' duty to apply for
    registration   5.4
  caution, entering of   8.2.1, 8.3.4
  charitable trusts, held on   3.3.4
  protection of purchaser   2.2.11, 8.2,
    8.5.3
  purchaser fails to pay money to two
    trustees
  trust for sale/strict settlement   8.2.1
  trust of land   8.2.2

Registered land *cont*
  restriction, registration of   8.2.1, 8.2.2,
    8.3.4
    charitable trust, and   8.6
Remainderman
  position of   6.2
  previous law   7.2
Rent, occupation   2.2.9, 7.5.1
  amount of   5.7.1
Resettlement   2.2.2, 3.3.8
Resulting trust   3.1
Retention of land   5.3
Reverter of sites
  no right of occupation for
    beneficiaries   7.5.1
  no consultation duty   5.7.5
Royal Assent   2.1

Sale of land
  court order preventing/enforcing   6.3
  trustee in bankruptcy's application,
    on   6.6
  duty to sell   3.8.3, 5.3
  inclusion of, advisability   5.10.4
  postponement, power implied into trust
    for sale   2.2.4, 3.6, 5.3
  proceeds, rights of person with interest
    in   6.2
  strict settlement, under (old law)   7.2
  trustees' power   5.3
  delegation of, old and new law
    5.8.2
Settlement, *see* Strict settlement
Settlor
  express power to appoint new
    trustees   4.3
  failure to appoint trustees   4.2
Strict settlement   3.3
  background   1.2
  charitable etc trust deemed (old law)
    3.3.4
  circumstances for   1.2.2, 1.2.3
  comparison with trust for sale   1.2.7
  creation after commencement of Act
    2.2.2, 3.2, 3.3.1
    exceptions to bar on   3.3.8
  deemed   3.3.1
  derivative   3.8.1, App III
  documentation   1.2.3
  effect of Act on   2.2.2, 3.3, 3.3.7
    new land brought in   3.3.8, 3.7.1,
    3.8.1
  exclusion from 'trust of land'   2.2.1

family charge, creation where land subject
  to   3.3.3
  inadvertent   1.2.3
  legal estate   1.2.2
  minor, conveyance to created   3.3.2
  opting out of SLA   3.8.1, App III
  power of sale, delegation under   7.6.6
  purchaser of land under   1.2.6
  sale of land under   7.2
  statutory owner   1.2.2, 1.2.3
  tenant for life, *see* Tenant for life
  termination of   1.2.5, 1.2.6
    ceasing to exist   3.3.7
    deed of discharge   8.5.1

Tenant for life
  challenge to powers   6.2
  death of   1.2.3
  powers   1.2.2, 1.2.3, 7.2
Tenant in tail
  instrument declaring, ineffective
    3.3.5
Termination of trust   7.8, 8.5
  beneficiaries' right   4.3, 7.8
  deed of discharge   8.1, 8.5.1, 8.5.3
  trust of land   8.5.3
  trustees' right   5.4, 6.5.3, 7.8
Third party
  donee of power of attorney, dealings
    with   2.2.6
  protection on delegation of trustees'
    powers   8.4
  statutory declaration from   8.4, 8.7.2,
    App III
Trust corporation   4.2
Trust instrument
  limitations on trustees' powers in
    5.7.1
Trust of land
  see also specific entries
  background, *see* Law Commission; Reform
  creation   3.2
  meaning   2.2.1, 3.1, 6.2
  termination, *see* Termination of trust
Trust for sale
  background   1.2.1, 1.2.2
  beneficiaries under   1.2.4, 1.2.5
  comparison with strict settlement
    1.2.7
  consultation duty, old law   7.2
  conversion doctrine, *see* Conversion,
    doctrine of

Trust for sale *cont*
  co-owners, where conveyance to   1.2.5
  creation after Act   3.2
  definition   1.2.4
  effect of Act on   3.2
  express   3.6, 3.8.3, 5.3
  implied   1.2.4
    effect of Act on   2.2.5, 3.7
  legal estate   1.2.4
  overreaching   1.2.5
  postponement of sale, power implied
    2.2.4, 3.6, 5.3
  statutory   3.7
  termination of   1.2.5
    purchaser, and   8.5.2
  trust of land, as   2.2.1, 3.1
  trustees' powers   1.2.4, 1.2.5
  use of   1.2.4
  wording, importance of   1.2.6
Trustee(s)
  appointment   2.2.13, 4.1–4.6, 4.9, 4.10
    additional   4.3.2
    beneficiaries' directions, at   2.2.13,
      4.4, 4.5, 4.9, 7.7
    court, by   4.4, 6.4
    exclusion of beneficiaries' power
      4.1, 4.10.3, 4.10.4, App III
    existing trustees, by   4.1, 4.4
    failure to appoint   4.2
    initial   4.2
    memorandum of, on conveyance
      4.10.2
    nominated person, by   4.1, 4.3, 4.4
    opting out of new provisions   7.10.2
    preconditions for new provisions
      4.1
    replacement   4.3.1, 4.4, 4.6
    subsequent   4.3
    written directions   4.10.1, App III
  beneficiaries, obligations to   7.6
  breach of trust   7.6.3, 7.6.5, 8.3.3–
    8.3.5
  capacity to be   4.2, 4.3.1
  consents, obtaining   7.6.3
  consultation by, *see* Consultation
  conveyance to beneficiaries   2.2.6
  corporation as   4.2
  court, application to   6.2
  death   4.3.1, 4.4
  delegation to beneficiaries   2.2.6, 5.8
    liability for   2.2.6
    see also Delegation

  duty to delegate   5.10.5, *138, 155*
  indemnity   4.8
  maximum number   2.2.13, 4.2, 4.4
  mental disorder   2.2.13, 4.3.1, 4.6
  minimum number   4.4
  minor   4.3.3
  powers, *see* Powers of trustees
  profit, may not make   5.7.2
  retirement   2.2.13, 4.7, 4.3.1, 4.7–4.10
    beneficiaries' directions for   4.7,
      4.9, 7.7
    court powers   6.4
    deed of discharge   4.7, 4.8
    exclusion of beneficiaries' power
      4.1, 4.10.3, 4.10.4, App III
    opting out of new provisions   7.10.2
    preconditions for new provisions
      4.1, 4.7
    protection on   2.2.13, 4.8
    written directions   4.10.1, App III
  valid receipt, number for   4.2
  vesting of property in
    maximum number   5.4
    new/continuing trustees   2.2.13, 4.7

University land   2.2.1, 3.2, 3.4
Unregistered land
  limitation in trust instrument, and
    8.3.4
  purchaser fails to pay money to two
    trustees
    trust for sale/strict settlement   8.2.1
    trust of land   8.2.2

Vesting order   6.1, 7.8, *see also* Powers of
  court

Will
  doctrine of conversion, and   7.4
  effect of Act on   3.7.3
  gift of residue   3.8.2
  minor appointed trustee   4.3.3
  personal representative, *see* Personal
    representative
  trust created pre-Act, no consultation
    duty   2.2.8, 5.7.5, 7.6.4
  'created by or arising under'   5.7.5
  transitional provisions   2.2.8, 5.7.5
  trustees appointed by   4.2